Touch a Butterfly

TOUCH A BUTTERFLY

Wildlife Gardening with Kids

April Pulley Sayre

ROOST
BOOKS

Boston & London

2013

ROOST BOOKS
An imprint of Shambhala Publications, Inc.
Horticultural Hall
300 Massachusetts Avenue
Boston, Massachusetts 02115
www.roostbooks.com

9 8 7 6 5 4 3 2 1

First Edition
Printed in China

∞ This edition is printed on acid-free paper that meets
the American National Standards Institute Z39.48 Standard.
♻ Shambhala makes every effort to print on recycled paper.
For more information please visit www.shambhala.com.

Distributed in the United States by Random House, Inc.,
and in Canada by Random House of Canada Ltd

Designed by Lora Zorian

Library of Congress Cataloging-in-Publication Data
Sayre, April Pulley.
Touch a butterfly: wildlife gardening with kids / April Pulley Sayre. —1st ed.
p. cm.
Includes index.
ISBN 978-1-59030-917-9 (pbk.: alk. paper) 1. Gardening to attract
wildlife. 2. Wildlife attracting. 3. Garden animals. I. Title.
QL59.S18 2013
635—dc23
2012021579

For Suzanne Fox, Frances Martindale, Ralph Wales,
and all my "wild family" at the Gordon School.

For Jeff, who planted the plants and daily reopens my eyes
to the business of bees and squirrels and birds.

Contents

Gardening for Wildlife

Are you *that* family? The slightly wild one, with wide-eyed, active kids, always into messes, ready to explore? Or do you dream of being that family, getting away from couches, televisions, and slightly over-tidied lives into deeper, goofier nature joys? If you seek wild adventures, there's no need to travel by car, bus, or plane to a faraway park. You can create an environment for nature adventures right outside your door. Even a small offering—a bowl of water, a flowering plant, a pile of sticks—may be just what a creature, nearby, needs. Your efforts can help that creature and bring it closer so your family can delight in seeing it.

Doable Projects for Backyard or Schoolyard

This book covers simple steps families can take to wildlife garden. Wildlife gardening is planting plants and building garden structures to create wildlife habitat. Habitat is an extended concept of home; it's not just a house, burrow, or nest. It includes all the conditions a creature requires to survive, including food, water, shelter, and a place suitable for raising young. In wildlife gardening, you'll try to provide as many of these elements as you can.

No vast country estate is required to provide valuable habitat. A yard or small courtyard can shelter and feed butterflies, lizards, quail, turtles, and a host of other creatures. A window box, planted with the right flowers, can be a feeding spot for hungry hummingbirds. Some schools have turned their inner courtyards into wildlife habitats by planting berry-yielding shrubs and nectar plants for butterflies.

Even if your neighborhood seems devoid of wildlife, with a little work your site can become a wildlife magnet. Build a water garden, and frogs and dragonflies are likely to show up. Plant caterpillar host plants, and butterflies are likely to arrive. Set a hose to dripping, and moisture-loving toads, thirsty chipmunks, and doves who need a drink are likely to stop by. A rooftop garden or an apartment porch in the middle of the city can host and feed migrating warblers and monarch butterflies. It's astounding how wild creatures, almost unseen, move through increasingly urban landscapes to find places designed for their needs. Is it the smell of a plant? The sound of water? Only the creatures, and perhaps a few scientists, know.

This book goes beyond conventional wildlife-attracting methods such as putting up bird feeders. The focus is natural support for wildlife: planting berry bushes, seed plants, and nesting trees wild animals need. The goal is to provide for wildlife in the most sustainable way possible—with native plants and structures that require little maintenance. Once you provide food, water, and shelter, creatures will begin to depend on them.

The Joy of Wildlife Watching

Wildlife gardening includes considering the whole range of wildlife needs—not just food sources but also places to find a drink, bathe, sun, cool off, survey the territory, and escape from predators. Watching wildlife is part of the reward for this work. So included in this book is information on how to get closer to wildlife—how to behave, and what to construct, so family members can safely observe creatures at close range.

While you benefit wildlife, you'll also help your family in more ways than you might anticipate. A recent study found that after just five minutes of doing light exercise outside in green spaces, people's self-esteem and overall mood noticeably improved. Apparently, being in habitats with not just green spaces but blue spaces— water—yielded even more emotional improvement in these studies. This was especially true for the very young, the elderly, and those dealing with emotional issues. Time out in nature changes our lives during our most vulnerable times.

Even before a child is old enough to hold a seed and plant it, or identify a bird, he or she can enjoy a wildlife garden. Venture outdoors with a baby on your back or in your arms. While you perk up in the fresh air, that baby is absorbing the sounds of birds, the smells of plants, the feel of breezes, the slant of the sun—and your pleasure in that world. Being introduced to the outdoors as part of happy, everyday family life surely makes a child more at ease and connected to nature, long term. The natural world holds joys, comforts, and learning moments that enliven every stage of childhood and family life.

A garden is also art. It is a living kinetic sculpture. Wind plays with trees, grasses, branches. Rain moves leaves and makes rocks shine. Thunder shakes. Sun bakes. You can have fun with these elements by attracting moving shapes and colors—wildlife! With a little work, your yard, garden, or even patio can host wild creatures that will bring laughter, curiosity, science, and art inspiration to your children's lives.

At the same time, you'll have the satisfaction of knowing you're helping nature. Each wildlife garden is a reservoir, a sanctuary where plants and creatures can survive and thrive in an increasingly urban environment. They say that if you build it, they will come. Nowhere is that truer than in wildlife gardening. Butterflies and birds are waiting for you. All you have to do is invite them.

From Our Garden to Yours

For twenty years we've been wildlife gardening—learning lessons from trees and roots, songbirds and squirrels. My husband, Jeff, for five years was the director of a major native-plant nursery that grew 350 species of plants. He grew and installed plants to restore prairies, savannas, and wetlands. So his work filtered into what we did. We went from a couple of daffodils and some Canada geese to a yard fluttering with more than forty species of butterflies, 137 species of visiting birds, and a water garden full of vocal frogs. Our faraway wildlife photos became close-up, dynamic photos because the animals became so acclimated to our part in their lives. Thanks to Jeff's work, we went slightly overboard, planting over three hundred species of native plants in a 1.5 acre suburban yard.

Wildlife gardening, of course, is a supremely local kind of work, heavily influenced by whatever sand, sun, and soil you have. So what I'm sharing here is what we've learned, bolstered by experiences from wildlife gardener friends around the United States and the views of experts mined from twenty years of researching and writing about nature. It is my hope that these suggestions will lead you to wildlife gardening practices, resources, and activities that fit your habitat. I've tried to choose activities that can be adapted to a wide variety of habitats. This book deals with attracting small creatures: birds, butterflies, dragonflies, native bees, squirrels, toads, and the like. If you are hoping to bring moose into your yard—um, consult some other text!

Even on the small scale, wildlife gardening seeps into all aspects of life. So I've shared a few personal anecdotes, as well as practical garden advice. Gardening has deeply influenced my work as a writer of books about nature and science for children. During school visits, thousands of educators and children nationwide have shared their thoughts on nature and gardening with me. That, in turn, has sprouted new books and garden ideas. Both writing and gardening return more to you than you expect. Most of all, they take their time—and, happily, they surprise.

Part One

UNCOVERING YOUR HABITAT'S POTENTIAL FOR WILDLIFE

It's tempting to start wildlife gardening in a garden store or home improvement store when you see seeds, shovels, or plants on sale. We all get excited at the possibilities. But if you can stand to wait, there's another way. Let the creatures show you what they need. You may already have habitat elements that, with just a little tweaking, can do a great job of inviting and hosting wild animals.

In this section are small, targeted explorations to help you connect with neighborhood nature—wildlife that already lives around you. Foxes, coyotes, skunks, and raccoons survive almost unseen in cities. Birders find rare migratory warblers in unlikely places, such as trees right outside office buildings and even at sewage ponds. The old adage "You see what you expect to see" rings true with wildlife watching. Even country dwellers miss many of the creatures that live near them if they haven't learned to tune in to the sounds of toads chorusing, sandhill cranes calling, or raccoons jabbering. So gather your kids and prepare to relearn a few skills our hunting-and-gathering ancestors honed. Let's meet the neighbors—the wild creatures around your home!

1 : THE COMFY SPOT

Every home has a favored spot: the edge of the couch, the wooden bench near the fireplace, the stool where the kids like to sit and spin. Wild animals have their favored spots, too. In our yard, cardinals, catbirds, and sparrows gather in late afternoon. They hop underneath the seat of the metal chair and perch on the metal table. They perch on the rungs of nearby tomato cages and on overhanging blackberry vines. Something here is comfy—for searching, for sunning. Birds pop up and down, stripping seeds from overgrown grass. Other birds settle in the sun. And there is a togetherness, of many species. When some find it comfortable and beneficial, others are drawn to the spot, too. Perhaps it's like a crowd of people that gathers, eager to see what's worth waiting for, what's on sale. Or is it safety in numbers? Who knows? Either way, finding the active spots, the "comfy spots," for wildlife in your yard can change how you garden.

Observing Activity

To discover these active spots, you and your wildlife "team" can take turns observing the yard. Set up a schedule. Observe the yard four times in the day: early morning, midday, late afternoon, and early evening. In our summertime yard, that would be 7 A.M., 12 noon, 5 P.M., and 8 P.M. Getting the time exact is not important. You are getting a feel for the yard. Family members sign up for shifts. (This is a good excuse for parent quiet time, by the way.)

This activity can take place over a day or a week. The main purpose is to spend some time watching what's going on in the area you are going to garden. Each watcher should bring a nature notebook and write down observations: wildlife heard and seen over fifteen minutes. What walks or flies across the field of view? Each watcher will need to be quiet. But scribbling in a notebook or drawing a bit are okay.

If your family has more time, try longer watching shifts. Watching absolutely intently isn't necessary. Low-key activity is allowed. It will take a while for wild creatures to settle down and return to their routines if they see you out in nature. Being present is the important thing. Spend an hour reading a book, lazing in a hammock, playing a quiet game in a screened porch where you can see the outdoors. What's essential is that you can see and hear what is going on.

Have everyone meet to share what they noticed. What do they wonder about what they noticed? Is there an area where creatures often gather? When and where do these gatherings happen? How might you add more of what is attracting them to that spot? Take notes so that you can incorporate what you've learned into your wildlife gardening plans later on.

Begin Your Family Nature Notebook

Create your own family nature notebook. Perhaps it's a scrapbook, or a box with individual notebooks for each garden helper. Maybe it lives as a nature folder on a family computer, as well. Gathering photos, recordings, and resources from your experiences as a family will help you draw satisfaction from the journey you're taking as wildlife gardeners. It's easy to forget how far you've come, what you've already accomplished in gardening. Photos and notebooks can help you see, and appreciate, all you've already done for the land. Looking back on this work will give your family smiles at accomplishments, and at the mistakes and lessons learned as well.

The Garden Photographer

As you start observing your space, document your garden process before you plant. Who's going to be the garden photographer? Ask for a volunteer. Help your young shutterbug to document the process. He or she should choose spots for before-and-after photos. Set a stake or a tag of twine exactly where the photo should be taken. It helps to lean against a fence, branch, or other landmark you can note. (Try to choose something that you plan to keep, whatever your garden plans.) Remember to mark how high the camera is, and in what direction it is pointing. Then the before-and-after shots will match more exactly—which makes the transformation appear even more stunning. You could also use a smart device, such as an iPad, iPhone, or other phone camera with a GPS, to mark the photo site.

2 : OPENING YOUR EARS

Sound is one of the first clues to the presence of wildlife. Wildlife tour guides—and hunters—typically hear animals before they spot them. In order to survey your habitat for wildlife, and research for gardening planning, your family will need to "look" with their ears. Do we really know how our yards sound?

Listening is one of the most selective activities done by our brains. In order to avoid bogging down our circuits with too much information, we unconsciously filter out sounds: noisy roads, busy motors, wind, bird calls, insects droning. Below is a listening exercise to help your family practice wider listening. It will assist you in beginning to document your habitat. One of the fun parts of wildlife gardening is not just before-and-after photos but before-and-after sound samples, as well!

Recording Nature

Set up two to five stations in your yard. Mark each of these spots with a stick, rock, chair, or whatever suits. Set a small recorder at each spot. It needn't be high quality. A tape recorder, digital voice recorder, recording feature on a phone—anything will do.

Split up your wildlife sound observers (yourself, children, and any aunties, uncles, and grandparents who want to join) among the sites. Have them sit quietly for six minutes while the recorders are running. The listeners' eyes should be closed except when they are writing down or drawing what they hear. As a family, look at the notes and listen to the recordings. Were there surprises? Things you did not realize were there?

Recording audio in your yard, or a park, can lead to new avenues in learning. There are a number of resources for discovering and identifying the animals that made the sounds you hear. The Macaulay Library of Sounds at the Cornell Lab of Ornithology (www.macaulaylibrary.org) produces CDs and downloads of sounds. Bernie Krause (www.wildsanctuary.com) and other dedicated recordists capture animal sounds all over the world, and you can purchase their sound recordings in many formats. It's great to have their sounds handy on portable devices for checking sounds in the field. Listen to these professionally made recordings, and you can learn animal calls and open up a new world for your ears. In years to come, as you install your wildlife garden, your yard will be filling up with new sounds—the sounds of birds, water, laughter, hummingbird wings—brought to life by your family's efforts. So keep those early "listening notes" and recordings.

If you have a hearing-impaired family member, he or she may still be able to participate, thanks to new technologies. As many people age, they lose their ability to hear high-pitched calls of creatures such as warblers. Regular hearing aids are geared for the middle-range pitches of human speech, not the high-pitched sounds of warblers and many other small wild creatures. But these days some hearing aids can be reset for higher pitches, such as those a person hears when out birding. Another alternative technology is Songfinder, a small handheld device that transforms high-pitched animal sounds into sounds that can be heard in normal ranges.

3 : GARDENING IN THE RAIN

One of my favorite garden moments came one evening when it was getting dark and I had a few more plants to put in the ground. I pushed on. The rain plip-plopped on my back, on my head. The air temperature began to drop. Soon my knees were muddy. The sky became the kind of dark that you are sure, from brightly lit indoors, is true dark. But I was outside, still animal, so my eyes adjusted. Toads I never knew lived near us hopped out to hunt. I smiled through rain dripping off my hat. The toads and I were fellow travelers, in kinship in some small way. I have rarely been happier than in that moment.

If your family is only observing your yard when it's midday, warm and sunny, you're missing half the fun. Weather, climate, and the seasons all impact the nature of your wildlife garden. For a better understanding of your habitat, seek some off times, less

comfortable times, for gardening. Just dress for the occasion. (Or prepare to warm up with towels and hot tea or hot chocolate afterward.) There's a lesson in savoring all kinds of weather. And in the garden, it can introduce you to animals and behaviors you would not see otherwise.

Rain Walks, Fairy's Washing Walks

To encourage your kids to understand the world wild creatures live in, the conditions they encounter beyond sunny summer days, try some walks at other times. Take your kids on a "rain walk" during or soon after a gentle rain when lightning is not present. Check out what the earthworms and birds do during this time.

Experienced wildlife watchers know that often it's the "bad" weather conditions that make it easier to see wildlife. On rainy, cool days in spring, migrating birds come down from the trees closer to the ground where insects are more active. At those times, you don't have to crane your neck to see them. Furry mammals, on the other hand, sometimes stay out of the rain altogether. (Although the squirrels do sometimes venture out, curling their tails overhead like umbrellas.)

Use this time, too, to learn more, as water detectives, about the wildlife habitat you are developing. Where does water puddle? Where does it pour? What happens to leaves when rain drops onto them? How do ants fare when huge raindrops crash into the dirt near their nests? Go out in the rain, open to seeing what it does. Let the questions and observations bubble up naturally. Don't bog down the experience too much with analysis or lesson plans.

Have your kids suggest and plan some other kinds of walks. They can plan the time and theme. For instance, they might schedule an early morning garden adventure to see what dew can do. Where we live it's moist enough for dew to collect on spiderwebs. They become jeweled, lace-like beauties whose folk name is "fairy's washing." (The fairies supposedly set their jeweled washing out to dry.) Another thing to observe is morning glories, which open this time of day. Mark what direction the flowers are "looking." Then check back. Are they still pointed that direction later in the day? What about other flowers in your family's habitat? Are there some that are only open in the morning, or evening, or perhaps at night?

Making Room for Mud

Gardening can be messy, especially when gardening in the rain. We all need an in-between, a place that does not have to be clean every second of the day, a place where projects and mess are loved. In my grandmother's house, my favorite spot was the "mud room." It had two sloppy sinks, the clothes washer, a few mats for boot stomping, and shelves of colorful canned pickles and beans. On hooks were heavy woolen shirts and six old-fashioned floral bonnets we wore for gardening. And even though Grandfather used it, it was Grandmother's domain, in some essential way.

Where does your family come and go? Where do you romp and stomp each time? Find out what entrance and exit give access to the garden. Think about which tools are most essential for you and your children. Search through the closets to find some old shirts, pants, and sweatpants to serve as garden clothes. They don't need to be washed every time. Now find a place: a mud room or mud corner.

Set up hooks for clothes. A bucket or a small table where things can be dropped and propped is a help. If you have several tools, put up a cork hook board. You and the kids can make a production out of deciding where each tool should be propped or hung. Just make the kids' tools lower and reachable. Secure sharp tools, and tools such as hoes that can fall over, with hooks to hold their handles.

For extra efficiency and fun, outline each tool with a dark marker or paint on the wall or cork board where it hangs. Each time, after gardening, little and big folks can make a game of finding where things belong. Find the shape of the tool, find its outline. You and your kids can look over the board for missing items. It's a surefire way to remind yourself that you left that trowel or clippers back in the hedge where you were working. That way they won't rust out in the rain until you remember them. (I can't imagine who might have done that—too many times.)

Cleaning tools is important. Tools will last longer if they are free of mud and moisture. So get a good stiff brush to clean off the metal ends. Hand tools can be stored in a bucket of sand. Teaching kids to care for, store, and clean gardening tools is one of the important lessons of gardening.

The mud room is an anchor for the new direction you're taking as a family. It demonstrates your commitment to your new practice of gardening—welcoming wild creatures, a little mess, and perhaps some muddy kids right into your life. It will help ease the transition from inside to outside to in.

4 : LAYER CAKE OF LIFE

As you were observing birds for "The Comfy Spot" chapter, you probably noticed that
some kinds of birds perch high up in trees, while others hop amid lawn grass. Still others scuttle beneath shrubs or choose the tangled, shady middles of shrubs. Their posi-
tions—high, low, exposed or hidden, shady or sunny—are not random. Each species
has general preferences for how high above the ground it spends most of its feeding and
resting time. Fish, frogs, and turtles also seek out layers in streams and ponds.

In the wild, the edges of ecosystems—where the forest meets field, or woods meets
stream—are often the areas with the most wildlife. Where ecosystems meet, layers
come together and hold many creatures. The key to inviting a variety of wildlife to your
habitat is to provide many layers—conditions that suit a variety of creatures. A layered
habitat is like a building with many floors and apartments, and thus, many homes. In the

wild, creatures often specialize in one layer or another, and thereby avoid competing directly for perches, food sources, and nesting sites.

So what kind of layers can a yard have? Look for variations, high to low. Trees, shrubs, low-growing flowers, and ground cover are layers. High walls, benches, stepping stones, and open ground are layers, too. On a porch or deck, hanging plants, potted plants on plant stands, and lower pots of flowers are layers on a small scale. They provide space for many different creatures to visit simultaneously without conflict. A yard with a water garden has additional layers: trees and shrubs overhanging the water, wetland plants edging the water garden, plants whose roots grow in the water but whose stems stick out, duckweed that floats on the water's surface, other plants and surfaces deeper in the water, where tadpoles swim.

Our backyard lawn became a layered habitat when we planted a tallgrass prairie patch. Cup plants, tapping into wetland water, grew tall. Shorter prairie monarda, rosinweed, leadplant, and other species created other layers below. Suddenly, migrating birds we'd never seen ventured into the prairie, close to our house. Both the prairie and the vegetable garden provided avenues that brought warblers, dragonflies, and other creatures from the stream and forest out into the main yard where we could view them.

A small vegetable garden adds layers almost by accident. It provides poles to climb, tomato cages to perch upon, and squash vines to scoot up and down. It forms

a tangled wonder world for wrens, tanagers, chipmunks, and hummingbirds. It has overlapping leaves for migrating warblers to check for caterpillars. Birds search every surface and, along the way, they remove garden pests. Consider all the layers a small vegetable garden has compared with the mowed lawn beside it.

Looking at Layers

So what layers does your space have? What layers do you want to create? Get your kids involved in studying your wildlife garden area with an eye to layers. One point of reference for school-age children is rain forests. Elementary school students usually study rain forest layers: forest floor, understory, canopy, and emergent layer. Point out that some versions of these layers are present in all natural landscapes—not just rain forests—and create varied niches. If you provide these layers in your wildlife habitat, creatures of many kinds will take up residence.

To get kids seeing layers, have them cartoon a picture of your yard. ("Cartoon" sounds more fun that what these images really are: diagrams.) Ask them to draw and label layers they see. Nothing needs to be perfect. Layers don't have to be the same size or of the same importance, because "layers" is a rather fluid term. A layer to a frog might be a tiny flat rock or a mayapple leaf. A layer to a deer might be a valley and a hill. Whether your kids see the backyard world on the scale of deer or moose or grasshopper—it doesn't matter. The point is to roughly sketch, label, and perhaps color possible layers in your yard. Then imagine what layers you might install. Then, get to work adding some layers!

If you aren't ready to plant, or it's not the right season, create structural layers just for experimentation. Put out a stick, a hook, a table, a sculpture, a small shrub, a chair—any kind of perch. See what creatures, if any, begin to use it. Add massive rounded or jagged rocks for perching, but also smaller flat rocks for creatures closer to the ground. Think creatively and have fun! You'll begin to learn what creatures already live in your area and how you might provide for them, long term. In later chapters, as you learn about specific plants that suit butterflies, dragonflies, berry-eating birds, and the like, keep this concept of layering in mind.

5 : OH, THE ITCHIES! BATHING, SUNNING, AND ANTING

Wild animals have needs beyond food, water, and shelter. They seek comfort and work on maintaining their overall health and appearance. They don't have hairbrushes and bottles of lotions, yet they find ways to clean off, soothe itchy skin, and comb their hair (fur). Part of the fun of wildlife gardening is noticing and addressing not just the big habitat elements but these incidental needs, as well.

To take care of itches, many animals use dust. Squirrels and other mammals roll in dirt. Sifting dirt through their fur dries and removes parasites. Typically, afterward, mammals bite, lick, and run their paws over their skin and fur to clean them. Birds use

dust baths, too. They also preen—stroking their bill along their feathers—to remove particles and straighten the feathers.

Below are some simple ways you can help wildlife, and keep wildlife in your yard, by providing patches of sun, sand, and exposed soil that animals can use for their dust-bathing. The extra payoff of these small efforts is that children get to watch animals occupied with these relaxed, sometimes humorous-looking comfort activities; they can relate as they learn their own routines for brushing, washing, and bathing.

Sunning Spots

Providing sunning spots is relatively straightforward. Rocks, bricks, and other items that warm up quickly and give lizards a good view of the surroundings are an excellent choice.

Dust Baths

As gardeners, we may want to fill every patch of dirt with plants, rocks, or organized pebbles. But leaving an area of dirt several feet wide for a dust bath really helps wildlife. If you don't already have a bare dirt area, scratch away some grass and plants to make an official "dust bath." Be warned, though, that wild animals don't always go along with gardeners' plans! Sometimes creating a dust-bath area means following the cues of the squirrels and birds who dig, gather, roll, and flutter. Their instincts about the dust-bath site may require a little adjustment in your garden design.

If you do have a bare dirt or sand area, your kids can have some extra wildlife fun. Have them hunt sand and dirt for the small pits built by larval antlion lacewings (also called "doodlebugs"). The antlion stays at the bottom, waits for insects to slide in, and then eats them. It's better than sci-fi, and kids love finding them.

The Anting Place

Blue jays, robins, and many other birds ant. The bird sits on an anthill or a dust spot and spreads out its wings. (This looks awkward, as though a wing is broken.) The bird's head may loll. Its feathers fluff. It may close its eyes and open its mouth as ants crawl through its feathers. What does this do? Only the birds know for sure. But scientists suspect the formic acid that ants make may help deter biting mites. Some birds actually grab ants and wipe them on their feathers. So ants in your yard may be an attraction. Keep some around!

We've also observed a grackle using a bit of orange rind for a similar purpose. (We put out oranges to attract orioles, catbirds, and red-bellied woodpeckers. These birds feed on the orange flesh.) One day we saw a grackle pulling off pieces of rind and stroking it through its feathers, much the same way birds do with ants. Was it using the acidic orange rind, or some of the natural orange oils, to anoint its feathers and deter pests? We found Internet accounts of others seeing birds displaying the same orange-anointing behavior.

6 : THE GREAT ESCAPE

If you put up a bird feeder, songbirds will come. Cats and hawks, intent on hunting those songbirds, may come, too. Adding habitat layers, as discussed in chapter 4, can help provide escape routes. But more targeted planning may be needed to give small creatures a chance in the struggle to survive.

Cats on the Prowl

Hungry stray cats hunt. A domestic cat with a hunting habit will catch and eat birds even if it has plenty of food provided by its owner. Today these wandering, non-native cats are far more numerous in suburban areas than any wild cat, such as a bobcat, would be. So their pressure on wildlife is considerable.

According to the American Bird Conservancy, "scientists estimate that every year in the United States alone cats kill hundreds of millions of birds and more than a billion small mammals including rabbits, squirrels, and chipmunks." Especially at risk are migrating birds; they show up at a yard after having flown hundreds or thousands of miles. They are exhausted and unfamiliar with the territory, and with the local cat. They are easy prey.

So if a neighbor's cat or a stray cat is hunting birds in your area, take action. Check out what the laws are in your area about cats running wild. Your local Humane Society may be able to help. (Our county has an ordinance against free-roaming cats: residents can call the Humane Society to pick up a free-roaming cat. They hold the cat for a certain number of days, call the owners if there's a tag, and put the cat up for adoption if it shows signs of being people-friendly.) For more information about cat issues, search for the "Cats Indoors" program run by the American Bird Conservancy. Outdoor cats can at least be kept inside during the peak of bird migration. Building lookouts and hideouts, as discussed below, will also help mitigate predation by cats.

Hungry Hawks

Hawks are a different story. They are natural, native, and wild. Some eat squirrels and songbirds. But although these predators need to eat, Jeff and I don't necessarily want to give them an unfair advantage over their prey at our house. (A bird feeder creates an unnatural

concentration of songbirds in a small area. A bird feeder is really a bird feeder, when it comes to bird-eating hawks such as Cooper's hawks and sharp-shinned hawks!) So in our yard, we try to give the songbirds a chance by creating clear views, lookout spots, escape routes, and hideouts.

Still, occasionally, a hawk swoops by and dines. It's not fun to see one of our usual songbirds become another bird's meal. But we consider it a privilege to see, and feed, such a beautiful, powerful predator. That said, if the hawk is taking too much advantage of our feeder and snacking left and right, we stop setting out seed feed for a few days. (Okay, so I've been known to walk out and wave away a persistent hawk now and then, just to even the stakes for the songbirds!)

Escape Routes, Hideouts, and Clear Views

How does creating garden layers provide escape routes for small mammals, amphibians, reptiles, and birds? A vine can become a highway for a squirrel dashing away from a dog. A row of tall, dense shrubs allows small birds to move along the inner branches of the shrubs, out of reach of cats and hawks. A dense prickly pear cactus is full of crevices where lizards, rabbits, and quail can scurry if a coyote is nearby. The roof of a gazebo can become a shelter where an animal can hunker, out of sight of a hawk scanning from above.

Hideouts are important. Again, creating layers—plantings and structures of different heights—will automatically help provide these spots. Bushes, trees, rock piles, stick piles, even clay pipes and decks create layers and avenues to escape predators. In the next chapter, we'll delve more deeply into building stick and rock piles for this and other purposes.

Yet layers don't always mean safety—because layers can also hide a hawk or cat intent on hunting birds, chipmunks, and other small wildlife. For safety, small animals need clear views of what is around them. This gives them precious extra seconds to scurry and fly to safety if a meat eater is in pursuit. In our yard we noticed that a cat with a hunting habit liked to hide behind certain branches and shrubs near the seed feeder. Then it would dash out and leap up on the feeder. We raised the feeder and removed those branches and logs, which blocked predators from the songbirds' view. The hawk, too, would hide just a few feet away from the feeder in a bank of shrubs. So whenever we see it doing that again, we make time to do some shrub trimming.

Balancing layers with the clear views that wild creatures need to see approaching predators is one of those

things you'll figure out as you go along. There's no formula for exactly what to do, because it varies according to the species in your yard and the individuals' habits— methods of attack and ways of fleeing. This is one case where you may want to cut back some layers around areas where wildlife concentrate in larger numbers. That could be a bird feeder, a bush laden with berries, or a bird bath. Ideally, a small animal would have a secure burrow at its back, yet a clear view of the open area where hawks and cats might approach. Achieving this kind of setup is part of the wildlife gardening challenge.

Animal Hide-and-Seek

Engage your kids' imaginations by playing animal hide-and-seek outdoors with them. Take turns being hawks, cats, and other creatures hunting prey. Where would you hunt? Where would you run? Where would you hide? Have them imagine they are smaller, fleet of foot, or able to fly.

Based on what the kids observe, provide lookout spots for wild creatures. (In the next chapter, by making piles, you'll work on hideaways.) Think creatively. A new tree can be a lookout spot. Yet a lawn chair, garden stake, or flagpole can also be a perch for a red squirrel, chipmunk, or wren. One red squirrel that spots a predator will alert all the animals in the area. Alarm calls are heeded by many species. (Our resident blue jay uses this to its advantage. It imitates the call of a hawk until the birds all scatter. Then it swoops in and gobbles up the bird seed!)

7 : PILE IT ON! SIMPLE SHELTERS

Prepare to pile. Building a rock, stick, or log pile is one of the best things you can do for wildlife. It's multipurpose, meeting the need for layers (creating niches for varied species) and addressing the safety issue discussed in the last chapter by creating a hideout for small lizards, chipmunks, and birds to escape predators. A simple stick pile shelters—creating spots for resting and nesting. Your pile shouldn't be terribly tidy or closely packed. A pile needs spaces. The best material is wood: logs, sticks, miscellaneous brush. However, if you don't have those handy, a pile of rocks, bricks, shells, old flower pots, or broken concrete slabs can serve. They'll all provide shelters. But wood has the added benefit, for some creatures, of providing food.

The Little Log Pile

Get the kids involved in building a small wood pile. If you want to add to the romance of it, name it. Frog fortress. Chipmunk castle. Toad abode. Turkey tower. Get creative!

The brush pile or log pile needn't be huge. A three-foot-tall one is helpful. But a small one-foot-tall brush pile, along a fence line or a garden spot, works, too. Stack the heavier items in the center and the lighter ones on top. Use a mixture of sizes of wood. Cross the sticks to provide nooks and crannies for creatures to live. Of course, it needs to be stable enough so it won't topple.

A year-round pile is best. But small, tidy yards can make do with seasonal piles. Stack up brush in the fall, when you're cleaning up the garden—even if you'll want it out of the yard next year. Leave the brush pile intact during winter, when animals most need shelter. Wait as long as possible in spring before deconstructing the brush pile. Moths may fly out. Toads may hop out. Then you'll know your brush has been a good overwintering spot for small creatures. Preferably, wait until your garden has grown up a bit, so that the new year's living plants can provide shelters for the creatures leaving your log pile.

Some homeowners make a seasonal brush pile six or so feet away from their bird feeders so songbirds have a place to shelter during blustery winter days. A discarded Christmas tree, out near the bird feeders, serves the same purpose. (Just keep an eye out for lurking cats that might learn to hide behind the pile and ambush birds. If a local stray cat learns the trick, you'll need to create another plan.)

If you have space, a long-term pile will yield even further benefits. Rot actually helps it, creating food for insects. We made a woodpile for firewood but never ended up using it. As years passed, and we learned what lived in the pile, we couldn't bear to sacrifice those creatures' homes for fire. Chipmunks lived in it. Okay—we could have evicted the chipmunks easily. We have them aplenty. But the residents we really loved were the green bees who made their homes inside a few of the logs.

If you haven't encountered green bees, keep an eye out for them. They are shiny, stingless, iridescent, and beautiful. Some have rust colors and yellows instead of greens. In our yard, they are the major pollinators of cucumber flowers and squash flowers, too. Thank you for the crops, bees!

Another favorite log pile visitor was a turkey. We live in a suburban neighborhood, yet one day a young male turkey showed up. Each day for weeks it sat on the log pile against our house and preened. It spent hours sitting and preening. Suddenly, I was inspired to write a children's book about turkeys—still working on that. Never before had we appreciated the hard work a turkey must do to keep all those big feathers lookin' fine!

If you are lucky, a snake may take up residence in your log pile. In most areas, garter snakes, black rat snakes, and other nonpoisonous ones will show up. (They're to be welcomed. They keep the mouse population in check.) Some of these snakes use piles for overwintering dens. Of course, if you're in an area with plentiful poisonous snakes, such as the desert southwest or sandy areas in central South Carolina, build the pile far from young kids' play spots, in the part of your habitat definitely deemed wild. The best thing to do, to avoid snake or scorpion bites, is to teach kids hand and foot awareness so they step carefully and place their hands carefully when they are sitting down.

8 : WHAT'S ON THE MENU?

Berries. Leaves. Nuts. Nectar. Tree bark. Slugs. Mushrooms. Grasses. They're all food for wildlife of one kind or another. The more variety of wild foods you provide in your wildlife garden, the more kinds of wildlife you'll attract. And because some animals require several different foods for a balanced diet, the variety you plant will also help keep them healthy.

As you build your wildlife garden, you'll be working to provide these wild foods in as many seasons as you can. But before you start digging out current plants, and planting new ones, see what your yard already has. What looks like a weed may actually be a wild native plant that is already furnishing important food for wildlife.

The Wild Restaurant

What wildlife foods are being served in the habitat you plan to develop? Find out. Kids are great at this detective work. They're eye level with many layers of life that taller grown-ups don't see. So gather notebooks, pens or pencils, and cameras if they're handy. But before your kids wander and look, remind them that wild animals can eat many kinds of berries, leaves, and fruits that make people sick. Not every blue berry is an edible-for-people blueberry. This is a search for wildlife snacks, not people snacks.

As a family, walk around your potential garden space to search for wildlife foods. Have your dining detectives sketch, photograph, or make note of the possible wildlife foods. Have them map out suspected food sources, even if you're not sure what, if any, animal is eating them. (Some ornamental, non-native shrubs are full of beautiful berries that never get eaten but just shrivel and die.)

Once they've noted a possible source, have them look for signs that something is eating: Bites out of berries. Sections carved out of leaves and bark. Shells of nuts and other leftovers from meals are clues.

Examine tree trunks and branches for holes about a quarter-inch wide, close together, in rows across and up tree trunks. Woodpeckers called sapsuckers tap these holes, usually in spring. They visit them periodically to sip the sap that fills the tiny wells. Like flower nectar, sap is sweet. (The sweetness of maple tree sap is concentrated by

boiling it—that's how we make maple syrup.) Mourning cloak butterflies, hummingbirds, porcupines, and even red squirrels sometimes sip or lick sap from trees.

Large concentrations of animal droppings may indicate a nearby food source. (A regular perch may also be the cause of the concentration.) So check above and beneath, in front and behind, the bird-dropping areas. When the normally whitish droppings of birds are gooey purple instead, a source of fruit must be nearby. Perhaps you have a shrub that is providing berries or a cactus providing fruit.

Plants, of course, aren't the only food for wildlife. Bones and feathers are clues that meat eaters are nearby. Perhaps you'll find owl pellets—cylindrical masses with fur and bones in them. Owls swallow prey whole, then, eight or so hours later, regurgitate (spit up) cylindrical pellets with the bones and fur they could not digest. (Hawks and possums also cough up pellets, but their pellets are not as uniform in shape as owl pellets.)

Wrap up your studies by gathering notes and photos of what you've found. Have your kids create and illustrate a food "menu" for what's available in your yard. If your kids are old enough to be foodies and like a little role playing, they can write fancy descriptions or pretend to be restaurant critics and "review" the restaurant that is your habitat. Save these notes in your wildlife notebook. In later chapters, you'll be installing more plants to supplement the food sources you found in your study.

9 : WATER DETECTIVES

When most people think of wildlife gardening, they think of providing wild animals with plants—shelter and food. But water is essential for wildlife. It is needed for drinking, washing, bathing, and, for frogs and toads, reproduction. Before you spend lots of time and money on a big water project such as a water garden, go simple. First, investigate your space to see what water you already have.

Gather your kids and grab your nature notebooks, pencils, and a timer. (Why pencils? Because scientists usually use pencils when they're in a humid environment or working near water. Pencil marks don't run as much as ink does when paper is moist.) If your kids are shutterbugs, they might want to bring digital cameras, too.

Explain that you're all going to be detectives. (You can help the little ones.)

Everyone has twenty minutes to spread out and look for water and signs of water in the yard. Detectives should look for drips, puddles, moisture. Any signs of water. All the detectives should write down or draw what they see. Pass out the nature notebooks and pencils. Start the timer. Let everyone get to work.

At the end of twenty minutes, gather to discuss what was found. You can also do something more formal, sharing what you've found by writing in the computer, on big pieces of butcher paper, or on poster board.

The Ways of Water

As you're making your water notes, consider the following three factors, which influence whether animals will use a water source. Have your "detectives" brainstorm about what might improve the water sources for wildlife in your area.

Water Quality

Obviously, chlorinated pool water isn't suitable for wildlife. Pool chemicals can be toxic to plants and animals. Animals need fresh water, but it does not have to be pristine or clear. What we might consider muddy water exists in nature and is used by many creatures. The important thing is that the water is free of harmful pollutants; motor oil running off driveways and pesticides used on lawns and garden plants are all no-nos in water meant for wildlife.

Water temperatures can vary. That said, a dark-colored bird bath in the sun can heat water to scalding temperatures in the southeastern or southwestern United States. So if you live in a hot spot, you may want to place water in lighter-colored containers and shadier areas. That will decrease evaporation, too, so you won't have to refill it as often.

Safety

Have you noticed how many nature shows about Africa are shot at waterholes and river crossings? That's where the drama is! Water attracts thirsty animals, and it also attracts the animals that eat those animals. Animals are vulnerable when they are distracted by bathing or drinking. Predators such as hawks or domestic cats hunt at backyard birdbaths. So make the space as safe as possible for drinkers and bathers.

Put birdbaths up on pedestals or six feet or so away from steps and thick brush where a cat can hide and pounce. Hawks will hunt—they need to eat, too. But if you have a hawk daily dining at your birdbath, you may want to stop watering the birds for a few days. Animals not only need to be able to see predators; they need to be able to hear them in order to run, hop, or fly away. So try not to locate a water source right next to a noisy air conditioner, generator, or street. Put it on the quieter side of the yard. (That's not always possible, but it's worth considering if you are just beginning your yard design.)

Access

Like people at a pool, wild animals make use of stepping stones and shallows. In fact, water only a few inches deep is great for birds bathing and chipmunks needing a drink. Entering a deep, steep-sided pool would require a dangerous leap for them to get in, and getting out could be tricky if the edges are slick. (By the way, if you do have a swimming pool for people, make sure there are places where wild animals that accidentally fall in can climb out. Even a bit of a pool liner or a pool toy, strategically placed, can give a frog or squirrel a place to scramble out.)

Having branches overhanging and slightly submerged in the water source is a big help to songbirds such as waxwings and cardinals. They perch on these branches before and after bathing.

10 : WOOING WITH WATER

One hot day last summer, I noticed that the squirrels looked overheated and thirsty. A stream was not far away. An old pool, covered by a sagging cover that had filled with rain water, was close by. These water sources existed within twenty yards of the bird feeders. Still, the squirrel looked—well, to my eyes—miserable. I put out a small plastic food storage container filled with water. I had no idea, at the time, what a hit it would be.

The squirrels drank. The cardinals sipped. The chickadees flew down to investigate. Birds began to take baths in this four-inch-by-four-inch, two-inch-deep container. It seemed to be more of an attraction, in some ways, than the seed. Soon, the plastic container, which we refilled twice a day, was dirty.

So I upped the ante. I put out another bowl—a piece of pottery I made. (Before you

think that I did this for beauty, let me explain that out of respect for the Earth, I no longer do pottery. I leave it to others who craft it far better than I.) I filled it with cool water from the hose and put it on the sidewalk, not far from the bird feeders. We have researched, planned, built, and planted many things over the last twenty years. But this bowl probably received the best immediate reaction of any wildlife effort! Now putting out fresh water in a clean bowl is part of our routine.

Making sure fresh water is available to the wildlife in your yard is easy. Plus, if you don't yet know a lot about the animals in your neighborhood, providing water can bring them in so you can see what creatures are around. Then you can research their other needs and help provide for them.

The Bowl or Bird Bath

Put out a small shallow bowl of water. See what animals take advantage of it. It doesn't have to be fancy or deep. A trash can lid will do. So will the saucer from a flower pot. Experiment with placing the water bowl in different places in the yard. See what spot is favored by animals. Then dig it into the ground or gravel, if you like. (This can make the trash can lid more cosmetically pleasing, if the rim barely shows.) Place pebbles in the lid or saucer to give birds different wading levels. If lots of animals use the bowl, commit to dumping out the water and putting fresh water in every day or so. If you can, scrub it weekly—with leaves, a brush, whatever is handy. If it

gets really grungy, scrub it and wipe or wash it with a solution of one part bleach and ten parts water. Rinse thoroughly.

Add a Sprinkler

If water supplies aren't tight in your area, set up a sprinkler. It takes only a few minutes. The sound of water sprinkling is a magnet for birds. A light, gentle sprinkle for an hour and a half will do. Any time of day works. But mid-morning and late afternoon seem particularly popular for orioles, cardinals, hummingbirds, and visiting warblers in our yard.

Many birds don't bathe directly in the spray. They flutter among the wet leaves. So make sure your sprinkler wets not only the lawn but vines and trees where birds can perch and flutter. Our sprinkler does double duty—attracting birds and watering our vegetable garden. The birds, especially the chickadees, take advantage of the many perches provided by the fences and tomato cages. Your first instinct may be to set the sprinkler in an open area, but birds and other creatures will more likely take advantage of it if it's wetting other surfaces and has plenty of safe perches in the spray, or just outside it.

Use a Dripper

If water is scarce in your area, consider a small drip spout instead. Check a wild bird/birders' supply store or a local garden center for small drip hoses. A hose dripping on soil or into a rocky area or ceramic flower pot bottom may seem unimportant. It's not! In the desert, it brings in beautiful wild visitors. (The Arizona—Sonora Desert Museum has such a tiny drip site, and it's the place where birders find the most activity.) If you have some old soaker hose, you can make a small hole in it to provide a drip spot. Or channel a natural drip of water from a faucet toward an area where it can puddle. If you're feeling really ambitious, look up "downspout garden" on the Internet and see what folks do with water filtering off their roof. These wet areas can attract wildlife, too.

Stepping Stones and Perching Sticks

If you have a small body of water such as a wildlife pool or pond, but the animals aren't gathering, you may just need to give them better access. A fallen tree in a stream, or an overhanging branch, is a magnet for bathing songbirds. If you have an extra branch, why not put it into the water, on its side, with branches sticking up? Birds often bathe in the shallows between the submerged branches. Then they sun and dry themselves on the branches that stick up out of the water. Place a few stones just under water. The birds can hop on the branches or stones when they are not bathing, in order to sun and fluff and dry their wings.

11 : CONSIDER THE WIND

If you live on the open plains or near a body of water, wind is probably a big part of your life. The rest of us may not notice wind on a daily basis. Yet it's important to soil, plants, and, of course, wild creatures. Wind blows soil, snow, and leaf cover away from one area and to another. Wind dries soil. Cool winds chill plants, wild animals, and people. Along the seashore, breezes bring salt spray inland, making the nearshore area suitable only for salt-tolerant plants.

Is wind always a nuisance? Not at all. Winds lift milkweed seeds upward, helping them fly farther. Wind piles up leaves that become shelters for overwintering moths and butterflies. Migrating birds use tailwinds to push them farther on their migration. Winds are Earth's atmosphere stirring. They bring weather and change and beauty to a wildlife garden.

Seeing the Wind

The habitat you are building can be a great place to greet, and learn about, wind. On a windy day, engage your children in observing the effects of wind. Peek out windows to see if there are any birds nearby. In what direction are they facing? Are their feathers fluffed up? Which way are the birds flying? Are they huddled against the lee side of the house, the side away from the wind?

Make it easier for your family to see the wind. Put up a flag or weathervane. Or simply tie a piece of raffia or ribbon to a post, and let it flutter. Experiment with different sizes of ribbon or cloth. It needn't be anything fancy. A new, bright, fluttering flag may scare away wildlife from the immediate area, at least at first. Most will get used to it. But after your wind study, you may decide to take down a flag or cloth if it's keeping wildlife away from your yard.

As a family, go on a windy-day walk. Perhaps carry ribbons so the kids can play with the wind and see in what parts of your habitat the ribbons flutter or fall flat. Are there buildings that funnel the wind, making it stronger in some parts of the habitat you are developing? Brainstorm with your kids about how this could impact your garden. (Wind can topple a young tree before it's well rooted. Wind may blow away mulch. A plant in a windy area will need more watering to get it established.) Take this into consideration as you plan.

As gardeners, you can play with wind. Plant native grasses and watch the wind move them. Plant a willow and see it swing its long willow arms. If you create a water garden pond, watch the wind stir its surface. Observe maple seeds whirl down from trees above. Contour the garden, building hills and hollows that form windy areas and protected ones, as well. If you live near a beach, just planting a small row of native grasses, shrubs, or flowers can provide valuable shelter for migrating animals escaping the wind.

Planting Windbreaks, Shelterbelts, and Hedgerows for Wildlife

Following the dust bowl years of the 1930s, when airborne soil from drought-stricken fields choked the skies, planting windbreaks became a national effort in the United

States. Windbreaks are long lines of trees and shrubs, often evergreens, planted to shelter an area from the wind. Shelterbelts are wider windbreaks, with at least ten rows of trees. In Britain, farmers speak of "hedgerows," rows of bushes and trees, usually along roadsides and fields. All these plantings are immensely helpful at blocking the wind and keeping a field's soil intact. Yet they're also a major boon to wild animals, which live in the hedgerows and move along, across the fields, via these sheltered tree and bush highways. Hedgerows and other windbreaks also help automobile drivers, by stopping soil and drifting snow from crossing roads.

Unfortunately, in the last few decades, as memories of the dust bowl days have retreated, many windbreaks have been cut down. In years when agricultural prices are high, farmers are tempted to cut down trees and bushes so they can earn money from an extra row or two of crops in a field. Yet as global climate change makes droughts and other weather extremes more common, these windbreaks, shelterbelts, and hedgerows will be more needed than ever. If you live in an area with wide-open agricultural fields, consider planting these windbreaks on your own property or helping a neighboring farmer do so. Contact the US Department of Agriculture's Natural Resources Conservation Service (formerly called the US Soil Conservation Service) for more information on windbreaks and shelterbelts. Such windbreaks can be built on a smaller scale in backyards and schoolyards, as well.

12 : WINTER NEST HUNT

Snow is a gift to wildlife gardeners. It not only waters the plants and protects them from cold; it also reveals as much as it covers. New snow can help you uncover the hidden life of your wildlife area.

During breeding season, bird nests are typically camouflaged—obscured by the leaves of bushes and trees. But in winter, many trees drop their leaves. When snow falls, blobs of snow build up on bird nests leftover from the summer. Once you spot your first, you'll notice many more. Suddenly, bird nests are obvious everywhere. The birds' family secrets are out!

Nest Detectives

After a snowfall, invite your children to join you on a "blob hunt." Don't tell them, upfront, why you are seeking blobs. Bring along nature notebooks, pens, and small cameras. Walk, or drive, and have your kids notice blobs of snow. Snow perches on posts, flows precariously over gutters, and accumulates in windblown piles. It's a marvel of climate and physics—perfect for inspiring drawings or photography.

Soon your kids will see blobs in the trees and begin to wonder. Don't spoil it by explaining too early. Let them puzzle out what these blobs indicate, why they form. Encourage kids to hike closer or use binoculars for a better examination.

Have your "blob hunters" (now "nest detectives") photograph, sketch, or map these nest locations and keep them in your nature notebooks. (That GPS on the phone or other device, although not necessary, can be helpful for noting location.) Next summer, look in these spots for new bird nests. Many birds will build their nest in the very same place, occasionally even on top of the old nest. It's fun to figure out certain birds' nest-building habits as you do blob hunts, year after year. Often you'll find hidden hummingbirds' nests you had no idea were there. All these clues will help you know what creatures live in your yard and give ideas about what improvements to make in your wildlife habitat.

Drawing, photographing, and mapping are the best ways to document the nests. If you physically mark trees

where nests occur with obvious paint or tags, other animals may notice. Egg-eating animals, such as raccoons, seagulls, and crows, are clever. Sometimes they'll figure out human markings and raid such sites for nestlings or eggs. You really can't blame them; they're just following the signs to easy food. This has happened to scientists who marked nesting trees they were studying.

Field Guides and Following the Seasons

My mother and grandmother both owned the *Peterson Field Guide to Birds of North America*. In the margins they wrote dates when migratory birds returned or when an unusual bird visited. The ritual of writing in the books and checking them was a family tradition. I loved leafing through them and seeing what would show up each year, and when. To this day, my husband and I make similar notations in all our amphibian, reptile, mammal, and caterpillar field guides. For twenty years we have also kept a running list of wildlife sightings in our yard.

In the dead of winter, we consult it and count out the months before warblers return and wildflowers bloom. As I write, I consult it for daily details of various months of the year. Keeping these kinds of nature records changes the way you see nature. Noting these facts adds an extra bit of celebration to the first frog calls, vultures, and robins of the year. Discovering, and experiencing, seasonal changes is one of the delights of having a wildlife garden.

To tie in your seasonal observations to those of others, check out the Annenberg Learner "Journey North" website, www.learner.org/jnorth. It's geared for classrooms but is intriguing for all nature enthusiasts. Its focus is phenology, which the site defines as "the study of seasonal timing of life cycle events." You can compare your notes on frogs, plants, butterflies, and birds in your yard with the site's mapped tracking of these creatures' activities.

As part of wildlife gardening, you'll also need to stock up on field guides. As you look for wildlife, and garden for wildlife, wildlife identification questions will invariably arise. Hit the bookstores and libraries. Make a field guide a birthday and holiday gift tradition. It's best to invest in ownership of these books, digitally or on paper, because they'll be some of the most used books in your house. Make sure you have at least one solid field guide for each major category: birds, insects, amphibians, and so on. Kenn Kaufman has made his field guide to North American birds available for Spanish-speaking populations (*Guía de campo a las aves de norteamérica*). A caterpillar field guide, such as the Peterson guide to caterpillars of North America, is invaluable because kids, close to the ground, are sharp-eyed caterpillar finders, and their curiosity about them knows no bounds. In addition to identification books, also add some books that cover life history and behavior in more depth. Kaufman's *Lives of North American Birds* and David Allen Sibley's *Sibley Guide to Bird Life and Behavior* are good starts in answering questions about nesting and bird behavior.

13 : SNOWY DAY SURVEY

Winter is a challenge for the garden minded, for the warmth-loving, and for folks who like their fingers in the soil. But snow can teach. After snow falls, take a snowy hike, ski, or drive. This is a time of uncovering secrets that will help you build better wildlife habitat. Yes, it takes a bit of gumption to go out in the cold. But dress yourself and the kids properly and go for it. It's time to make tracks!

Snow Trackers

Snow reveals so much about the daily habits of winter-active animals. Search in snow for animal tracks. Draw them. Photograph them. Bring along a field guide to tracks,

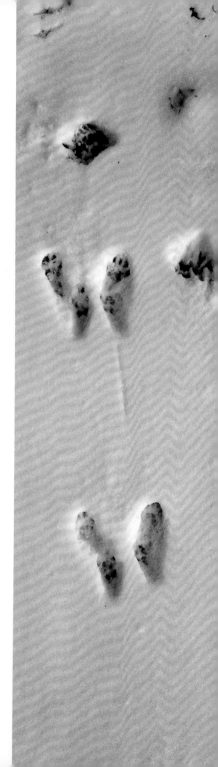

if you can. There are plenty of excellent books of this sort.

After your kids have puzzled through what animals made the tracks you found, don't let the fun end. Have them puzzle further. What were the animals doing? Where did they go? Back inside, have them draw, describe, or write a scene they imagine, based on the tracks. Learning animal tracks and imagining what animals are doing will increase your kids' sensitivity to the activities of nearby wildlife. This will give you hints about how to refine the wildlife garden you are creating.

Make Your Mark!

Following animal tracks with a truly skilled tracker is astounding. The depth of the imprint, the angle of the imprint, the position of the front to back tracks give knowledge that others cannot see. If you have a chance to get your kids out to work with such a skilled tracker, certainly do. (Check for workshops at local parks and Audubon education centers. Read tracking books such as those by James C. Halfpenny.) But a tracker's knowledge doesn't come only from telling and looking. There's another way to embrace your natural tracker. Experiment with your own two feet.

The physicality of hopping, jumping, and running and making tracks can't be beat. So if you're lucky enough to have snow, or live on a beach or near a muddy but safe spot, learn tracking by leaving tracks! Carry a pile of shoes, boots, even ski poles outdoors. Have your kids first try making tracks with their regular shoes. They should make some while walking, running, hopping, stopping, standing, and so on. This is practice time.

Next, take turns sending a leader to an open area of snow to make tracks while the others aren't looking. Then send out the trackers to study and see if they can guess a verb for what the track maker was doing in each part of the trail. The tracker can confirm or deny what he or she was doing.

Add a little wildness, if you like, by offering the options of other kinds of shoes, boots, or athletic gear such as snowshoes or skis. There's no end to the creative possibilities. Don't have snow, sand, or a safe muddy spot? Some wet or muddy shoes and a dry concrete sidewalk can be a start for your young trackers' abilities!

Seek Other Signs of Wildlife

Of course, tracks aren't the only sign of animals in the area. As a family, listen and look for the signs of birds: songs, eggshells, bones, nests, tree cavities, feathers, seeds, droppings, or pellets—the leftover fur and bones coughed up by owls and hawks digesting food.

Look for the signs of mammals: fur on a fencepost or another rough surface, droppings, nut shells from feeding, burrows, and so on.

Look for the signs of reptiles and amphibians: burrows, skins, bones, tracks.

Fish such as bluegills dig nests by fanning their fins to clear a pit of sand. These can be found on the edge of a stream or pond.

Use your nature notebooks and cameras to record what you find. It's likely you'll discover clues that will keep your nature detectives busy for quite some time.

Part Two

SETTING THE STAGE FOR WILDLIFE: PLANNING AND PREPARING YOUR GARDEN

If you worked your way in order through part 1, you've studied the wind, water, and ways of your yard. You've started a few small wildlife gardening projects. You've surveyed what you already have, begun to connect with the creatures of your yard, and perhaps picked up a few clues about what they need. This section is about laying the groundwork for bigger plans. It's about looking at the surrounding landscape, preparing the ground, and planting trees, shrubs, and cacti that have long-term benefits for your family, wildlife, and future generations.

14 : PLANNING YOUR GARDEN

You can certainly create a beautiful wildlife garden with small, impulsive projects. But planning, longer term, can be fun and rewarding. It can save time and money spent on structures and flower beds you later have to eliminate. Gather your wildlife gardening notebooks, with all the notes you took in your part 1 investigations. These will help you in your planning.

How you create your plan depends on your children's ages and abilities. Computer programs for landscape gardening can work. But graph paper or big poster board and markers can serve well, too. First, you'll need to map in the long-term structures: large trees, the house, shed, property boundaries, fences, permanent sidewalks, and so on. You can use online map sites such as Google Maps or www.nationalatlas.gov to find your

property and print out an ærial view. You can then use that to trace your house and existing landscape features to aid in your planning.

Make sure to include water sources. You don't want to plan your garden and then find it's nowhere near the water faucet and hose. You can dream big, and adjust your dream, by creating and moving adhesive notes, felt pieces, or whatever other art materials inspire you.

And there are other ways to imagine your garden. One summer, Jeff let an area of the lawn grass grow. Then he mowed curved shapes. Left behind were taller grass slivers and crescents—future flower beds. Over several months, he adjusted and refined his garden plans by remowing. Finally, when his plan was made, and he had time for gardening, he removed the tall-grass sod bits and created our formal butterfly garden.

Hands-On Planning the Wildlife Garden

You, too, can amaze friends and family with creative doodling on a large scale—with mowers, rocks, bricks, long stems of grasses, and more. Don't worry; you can erase it. That's the charm of outdoor mapping with hands-on materials. This way of planning gets the youngest wildlife gardeners involved.

The first step is to have your kids gather materials to symbolize, or mark, spots for gardens, trees, and the like. Sticks will do. Rocks will do. Garden stakes or sand or chalk or a raincoat or a giant leaf or a long string will do. Markers are only limited by your family's imagination.

Make it a game for the youngest. Have them choose the symbols for things you're planning to install: a butterfly garden, a water garden, a sitting spot, big rocks, and so on. Set a timer and have them run out to place these where they imagine them. Then they can explain their vision to the rest. Each child, and grown-up, gets a turn. Negotiate and adjust the final placement of the symbols and you've got your wildlife garden plan. Take a photo to remember what your family envisioned.

Call before You Dig! 811

If you're reading this book, then chances are you'll be digging in dirt soon. So before your dreams, ambitions, and shovels start chopping into soil, make a call. In the United States, a new nationally mandated phone number, 811, will get the local utility companies out, for free, to mark underground power lines and pipes you need to avoid, so you won't accidentally dig into a gas line, phone line, water line, and the like. Even if you think you're not digging soon, trust me, once the fingers get itching to plant, it's hard to stop them! It may take a couple of days for these services to come out and get their work done. So make the call soon, as you are beginning your garden dreams.

15 : GOING TO THE MAPS

Now that you have a good understanding of your immediate yard, investigate the surrounding land. Where do you really live? Habitats nearby will influence the success of the garden you create. By connecting your wildlife gardening to the greater landscape, you channel wildlife into your yard. Even more important, you can help address the greater region's wildlife needs, thereby maximizing your garden's benefit to wild species.

Where Do You Really Live?

As a family, set out to familiarize yourself with where you live. Walk or drive to a lookout spot where you can better see the valley, mountain, island, or whatever you live on. (In some areas, a tall building may be the primo lookout spot.) This is a good excuse for a road trip, a hot air balloon ride, or a hike in a nearby forest, desert, prairie, or mountain. Have your kids take photos. Ask your child or a tech-savvy teenager to introduce you to Google Maps and Google Earth to zoom in and zoom out on your landscape. Get a sense of your landscape in the bigger picture.

Animal Highways

Whether you're seeing the landscape in person or on a map, look for evidence of highways—pathways the animals might take. A wild animal pathway isn't exactly like a human one. (Although deer, moose, foxes, peccaries, and bears will certainly use man-made gravel paths and roads for ease of travel, at times.) Think more broadly of how and where animals might travel. Below are some ideas for animal pathways you might see. Once you recognize these, you and your wildlife helpers can help provide more pathways to make bridges between those pathways and the food, water, and shelter in your yard.

Hills and Mountains

Mountain ridges may bring migrating hawks to your land. As wind hits the side of a hill, it deflects upward. Hawks and vultures use this upward-moving air for a free lift, then soar as far as they can.

Seashores and Lake Shores

Seashores and lake shores are pathways for migrating songbirds, hawks, eagles, vultures, ducks, loons, owls, and cranes. Some birds stop and feed near the shores before crossing. So plantings here can be tremendously helpful to wildlife. Even a few bushes or native plants may be a welcome shelter for a bird that has flown hundreds of miles in the night. Clouds of migrating dragonflies are also seen at hawk-watching spots along mountains, seashores, and lake shores. Check with local naturalists or online to find out if there are any bird observatories and hawk watch sites that you can visit; the folks there should have a great sense of the landscape and what moves through it.

Streamside and Riverside Lands

A stream is a highway for much more than fish. A stream edged by trees, bushes, and wetland plants is a channel for frogs, dragonflies, minks, muskrats, and birds to travel through an urban area.

Shrub Borders and Tree Borders

Animals that live in trees and shrubs often avoid moving out into the open where food is scarce or a predator such as a hawk might find them. Birds, geckos, and frogs hop along near bushes and trees. These so-called edge habitats are rich with wildlife, because they are pathways for animals and sources of food and shelter. This kind of shelter is important, especially if you live on a lake shore or seashore, where animals rest and travel during migration.

Railroad Lines and Waste Areas

Don't write off the "waste" areas—the seemingly messy spots near where you live. Ecologists in the Midwest check along train tracks and roadsides looking for rare prairie plants to gather seed. It's a dangerous place to wander, and they do it with great care because in these forgotten areas many rare plants still hang on. These areas haven't been overtaken by lawn grasses and imported shrubs. Railroads are corridors for wildlife, in between train schedules. The same is true of hiking paths and walkways. (Many old railway lines have become hiking paths because of the efforts of organizations such as the nonprofit Rails-to-Trails Conservancy.)

   If you live near a creek, stream, pond, seashore, or patch of forest, all you may need to provide is a pathway into your yard. That could be a row of shrubs, trees, or flowering plants. Think of channeling the animals into your habitat areas. This action may bring wildlife and wild colors into your yard for better viewing. You can be a bridge between resources animals need, instead of a dangerous gap they might never cross.

Mapping with Kids

Once you have some sort of sense of the landscape from your lookout adventures and online map searches, have your kids map their place in the landscape. With younger children, these maps might be big, free-form drawings on poster board or butcher paper. Their concept of where they live—not just a house but in their neighborhood, complete with animals—could be fun to construct. Or create the maps on a smaller scale, using animal stickers to help mark possible animal pathways.

Older kids might want to do a more complicated concept, marking features on plastic laid over a photo or an online map. This could be done digitally with a design program. Thinking about where we live in the world is a great jumping-off place for reports, essays, and other such activities for homeschoolers. (Just imagine all the prepositions and geography you could fit into such a piece of writing!) Or they could create a scrapbook, each page connecting them to another aspect of what is around them, in the human and natural world.

16 : SOUND AND SPACE

The gurgle of water. The chirps of birds. The squish and scoop of kids shoveling dirt and sand. The snooze of sleepy parents in hammocks . . . yes, dream on! Gardens are full of acoustic possibilities. Imagine them.

In gardens, people seek what they don't have elsewhere in their lives. So if you have a noisy street and busy life, you may want a garden spot for quieter reflection. Some neighborhoods, though, are too quiet—rather sterile, with quiet houses where no one ever comes outside, and flat, mowed lawns where nary a creature chirps or squeaks. In this case, maybe you need a bit of garden sound to enliven your brain. You can, in fact, design your garden to have a sound flow—places of rest and places of noise. You can do this with wildlife in mind.

In chapter 2, "Opening Your Ears," you surveyed the sounds of your yard. Now it's blue-sky time. As a family, do a brainstorming session about what you would like to hear—or not hear—in your future garden. Build this into your plans.

Think, also, how your sounds will spill into other people's yards. The sound of wind chimes is lovely. For ten minutes or so. We had a condominium neighbor who walked out on the porch, hung up wind chimes, smiled joyfully, and then walked back inside where she would not hear them, leaving the rest of the world to listen to those wind chimes. Hourly. Daily. Incessantly. Bug zappers are another irritating noise—especially because they indiscriminately kill beneficial insects.

Sounds impact more than people. Birds compete with neighborhood sounds to make their voices known. In urban areas, with increasing sound, some bird species are shifting the pitches at which they sing to find an "empty" pitch range not filled by city noise. They're also shifting the times of day they sing. So the next time you hear a mockingbird singing awfully early in the morning, or even in the middle of the night, don't blame the bird. It may be humans at fault—because the people are making a racket all day long and don't leave space for the animals to get their messages (songs) out as well!

Creating a Quiet Environment from a Noisy One

Entire books have been written about how to garden in small city lots, and how to shield homes from noise. We won't cover all of that here. But, suffice it to say, for the purposes of wildlife, natural plantings and garden structures that buffer sounds are likely to have the most wildlife benefit.

Evergreen trees are wonderful for sound buffering. Evergreens also provide shelter for wildlife in winter because they do not drop all their leaves in fall. (They drop their leaves, called needles, more gradually, over time.) Many evergreens have seed-filled cones or small berries that help wildlife, as well.

Another good sound barrier is a berm—a raised area of soil. This takes quite a bit of space, but it has an added benefit. It offers additional growing space and new levels for your yard. These sound barriers are also good for shielding areas from wind.

17 : SENSING THE SOIL

Before you go in search of garden plants, you'll want to know what kind of soil you have. Certain plants do best in well-drained, sandy soils. Others flourish in moist, heavy soils that hold water well. Soil is made of air, water, rock (minerals), and organic matter—the remains of dead plants, animals, and other organisms. Soil is also full of living microbes that help plants grow. Soil anchors plant roots. It feeds plant roots. So its consistency is crucial to your growing plan.

　　Not all soil is created equal. When developers build homes, they sometimes scrape off the top layer, the rich topsoil of the site, and sell it. (Heavy construction compresses and damages some of it, anyway.) They do their building, fill in areas with cheaper soils, roll out grass, and call it a yard. What's underneath the turf could be anything. Hard

clay. Sand. A jagged mixture, with rich patches where it's easy to grow plants, and other areas that seem like desert. The soil may need nurturing. So take time to check out your soil. You and your young garden helpers can have hands-on fun and science observation along the way.

The Squeeze Test

Prepare for muddy fingers and perhaps some muddy knees with this project. Bring along nature notebooks and a small shovel or trowel. Using the trowel or shovel, dig up a few cups of dirt. Have your young gardeners each pick up a handful. Have them examine it. What color is the dirt? Color indicates some of the minerals in dirt. Reddish or pinkish dirt may contain a lot of iron.

Are there earthworms? That's a good sign. Gently pull those out and let them crawl along the ground. Keep the rest of the dirt. Everyone should have a handful. Next is the squeeze test. Each child should gently squeeze the dirt.

Does it hold its shape, as a lump in the hand? That means it probably has lots of clay.

Does it fall apart, sifting and sliding off fingers? Then it is sandy soil.

Press the lump of dirt. Does it crumble, not like sand but in lumps? It's likely loam, a good mixture of sand, silt, and clay. So it should be very good, in texture, for growing.

Write down in your nature notebook whether you have clay, sand, or loam at each garden site you want to plant. You could also add photos, or bring a soil sample to a garden friend or local garden center if you want confirmation. It is important to check the soil at various levels, as the quality can change with depth. The depth to which you dig will depend on the types of plants you are planning to install.

Let's Percolate!

The squeeze test you and your helpers have done tells about the texture of the soil. But what about its drainage? Lots of plant labels say "well-drained soils." What that refers to is how fast rainwater drains out of the soil. Gardeners often put it this way: Some plants like wet feet. Some plants like their feet dry. Like houseplants, outdoor plants can become soggy and rot if they are in the dense soils. On the other hand, plants in sandy soils can lose water quickly even if you water them a lot, because water quickly flows downward, out of reach of plant roots. The following percolation test can tell you what kinds of soils you have.

Dig a foot-deep hole in the area you want to plant. Make it a half foot wide or so. (You may want to dig these holes in several parts of the yard. Remember, soils can vary in your space.)

Use a hose or bucket to fill the hole with water. Note the time. Keep checking back, every fifteen minutes or so, to see how long the water takes to drain. If it takes several hours, you have poorly drained soil. Sandy soils may drain in only a few minutes. Now you understand what your plants are dealing with when it rains, or when you water the garden. Will the water stay in the soil long enough for the plants to absorb it? Will it stay in the soil so long that plants may rot?

Soil Testing with Laboratories

You and your kids have examined the basics of your soil. Now you can proudly tell other gardeners whether your soil is clay, sandy, or loam, and whether it is poorly or

well drained. (Soil talk is big among gardeners; they talk about it with the same likes, dislikes, and fervor that kids do about school lunch offerings.) A laboratory test can yield additional valuable information.

Your local agricultural extension office may offer soil testing, or at least the names of companies who do this. A soil test involves digging up a small cup of soil and sending it off to a lab to find out what is in it. (See the lab's information sheets or website for instructions on how much soil is needed and where to dig it from.) A standard nutrient analysis will test for pH, lead, texture, organic matter, and nutrients such as phosphorus, calcium, magnesium, potassium, iron, copper, manganese, zinc, boron, and aluminum. Some garden centers offer home test kits for pH, so if you have budding scientists at your house, you may want to try that test.

Who cares about all this detailed soil information? Careful gardeners who want to ensure success care. Admittedly, I've gardened for years in places without getting around to doing soil testing. But, then again, I've spent hundreds of wasted dollars in plants that I set in soil that was totally inappropriate for them. Trial and error are expensive in time and money. I don't follow cake recipes well, either. So learn from my bad example. Test the soil and save yourself money and annoyance.

"Fixing" Your Soil

If your own tests and laboratory tests indicate your soil is lacking, in nutrients or texture, there are ways to change it. For instance, you can add organic matter—compost, shredded leaves, and such—to help build the soil texture, so it holds water longer. Clay soils may need breaking up, with shovel work and the addition of sand and compost to change their texture, as well. Try to avoid purchasing peat, which many garden books recommend as a soil addition. Peat may help your garden, but it's being mined from precious wetlands at an alarming rate.

Ask a local organic gardener about how to build good soil. They'll have ideas about what works well for soils in your area. (There are as many tips and tricks for soil amendments as there are for creating the best barbecue!) Subscribe to magazines such as *Organic Gardening* and check out books and websites. You'll find a wealth of information about soil care.

Or, just keep your soil as is. There are plants adapted to almost every kind of soil. If you have sandy soil that drains water quickly, you can choose plants that like that soil. After all, even a sand dune can have grasses growing on it. The same goes for wet soils. Mosses, mints, cup plants, cardinal flowers, all manner of wetland plants can do well in perennially wet soils. As long as you know your soil, you can make smart garden choices.

Soil Care: Don't Tread on Me!

Healthy soil has air spaces in it. Water trickles through these spaces. Microorganisms, which are part of healthy soil, live in these spaces. To care for soil, avoid compacting it—squashing the air spaces out of it. As much as possible, try not to run heavy machines over it. Obviously, you and your kids can step on the soil when you need to, when you are gardening. Animals in nature do so without ruining it. Just don't pound it daily. In a small yard, a patch of dirt that is frequently trampled can become compacted, which will make it less apt to support some kinds of plants.

18 : THE LESSONS OF COMPOST

Witnessing old smelly glop becoming fresh, good-smelling soil is a revelation. It entertains young and old. Good compost is helpful not just for vegetable gardening but also for wildlife gardening. Best of all, compost has earthworms—squirmy, wormy lovelies that young children enjoy.

You don't need anything fancy to begin composting. Compost, of course, occurs in nature without human assistance. Tree leaves in a forest decay to become mulch, and then, soil. The pile of leaves we rake each year becomes terrific compost, after a few years.

But you can become more active in composting by starting an official compost pile. It's no more than a pile on the ground. Four feet wide will work, but any size that

accommodates your yard clippings and vegetable scraps will do fine.

If you have a small urban yard, you may want to hide your composting in a bin made of old palettes or wire. Fancier composting bins and barrels can be purchased. Check the Internet and magazines such as *Organic Gardening* for more information about composting.

Whatever your pile, the composting principles are the same. It's the mix of materials that will lead to successful compost or a smelly mess. Go for one-third greenish wet materials: grass clippings, fresh leaves and stems from plants, animal manure, or discarded vegetables from the kitchen. Add two-thirds brown, drier materials such as dried leaves, cornstalks, straw, or dry branches. Layer these materials, along with some soil as starter material. That soil should have microbes and earthworms to get your pile going. Of course, these will also move up from the ground into the pile if the pile is built on fairly good quality, living soil.

Compost piles need air and water. Folks in dry climates occasionally cover their piles with tarps to keep the moisture in. But with all the "green stuff," it's rare that a compost pile dries out. More often, a compost pile is too wet. Some gardeners may need to cover the top with a lid, plastic, or some other materials, to keep out heavy rains. Be sure to add enough "browns" to keep the compost pile moist but not sodden.

Air, too, will keep the composting process working properly. Layering sticks into the pile, and air spaces between leaves, helps the pile's microbes to do their work. You may need to stir the pile or turn it over with a pitchfork every few weeks to help the mix. If the pile smells stinky, that's a sign that it needs more air or more "browns." A fluffy, mixed pile is best.

The composting process can take several months. As the material decomposes, the pile will settle and decrease in size. The bottom of the compost pile will yield the new, rich, fluffy soil. You can dig down to reach this material. Or you may want to start a new pile, so that you'll have one fully composted pile to use, without the uncomposted bits of veggies mixed in.

Welcome, Volunteers!

In spring and summer, send your young gardeners to check the compost pile for "volunteers." These are plants that pop up from seed without your planting them. Expect lots of tomatoes—their seeds survive well. Transplanting these to your garden is a fun activity. You never know quite what these plants will yield. Seeds form from cross-pollination, so you may receive many color, size, shape, and taste surprises!

19 : PREPARING THE GROUND

I'm a shovel-a-day gardener. Bit by bit I accomplish projects. This suits my flexibility of time and inflexibility of body. It's better for me to do a little bit every day and not strain too many muscles and injure shoulders and knees. My sisters are get-'er-done gals. They charge in, dump supplies, mobilize every child and unsuspecting relative or friend into helping, and slam out that project by working late into the evening until everyone is tuckered out. Either method works. How you choose to prepare your wildlife gardening beds will impact whether it's a mountain of short-term work or a long-term maintenance project.

Making a Ground-Clearing Choice

If you're starting from lawn to create new beds, how do you clear the ground? Yard size and your energies should factor into your decision. Here are a few pointers regarding each option.

Interplanting

This method involves planting your new plants smack dab into whatever you've got, whether that is lawn or previous garden bed. Many native and wildlife garden plants are strong, so some will survive. But it's definitely taking a risk. We had a scrabbly-looking lawn and wanted to create a prairie. So we simply dug hundreds of holes right in the grass and plopped in small "plugs," rooted plants. Prairie plants vigorously root, in general. So some of the plants grew well. Cup plants, goldenrod, and monarda dominated. But columbine and more tender prairie natives eventually died out, crowded by the lawn grass or the expanding cup plant clumps. If we had it to do over, we'd likely dig out the grass cover and plant directly on bare dirt to make a more even prairie cover. What we wouldn't do is use Roundup or similar foliage killers, because our yard is near a creek and we don't want to pollute the stream water.

Whether interplanting works for you depends on what kinds of grass you have growing in your lawn. Many lawn grasses will die out. Vigorous grasses such as cheatgrass or zoysia may hold their ground against the native plants.

Burn

A controlled burn will take the surface grass and weeds off a patch of ground. But burning should not be taken on lightly. It can require a fire permit, protective clothing, and a good water source at the ready in case things burn too hot. Wildlife managers, who burn large areas to create prairie and savanna, have special training to carry out their work. Burning can give your new plants a head start, but the roots of many old plants, including strong yard grasses, will survive and pop back in a few weeks. So it's only temporary. It is less of a preparing-ground strategy and more of a method to maintain wild areas that are adapted to fire. (Some plants actually need fire for their seed capsules to pop open and deposit seeds.)

Smother

The smothering technique involves covering the area you want to garden with plastic, lots of dead vegetation, newspapers, soil, or a combination of these. This "no dig" technique allows you to smother the grass and weeds underneath and just begin your new bed right away. At first the beds you create will be slightly mounded up, but eventually, all the smothering material (except plastic, of course) will rot down to approximately soil level. The success of the technique, like the others, depends on what plants you are trying to smother.

Testing the Methods

Have your kids experiment with different ways of smothering lawn areas in small patches. They can brainstorm what to use. A spare board, a rock, a sheet of dark plastic, a sheet of light plastic, several layers of newspapers, some fencing, a leaf pile, a layer of soil are among the many options. Leave one section of lawn uncovered as a control. Then set up the other covered areas.

Have the kids check on them and note the appearance of the grass under each kind of covering each week. (They can take photos if they like. Mostly, they are learning to observe and gather data.) When a month or two has passed, and some of the patches seem dead, uncover the grass for further study. Your young experimenters should use trowels to slice out sections under each covering to see which methods squelched the grass. Then, leave the covers off and have them check in a week, then two weeks, to see which patch's plants are growing back the quickest.

20 : TRANSPLANTING TIME

Our neighbor had good intentions. When he learned that the plants he wanted to get out of his flower bed were beautiful redbuds, he decided to save them. He was eager to get the thing done. So he did. That very day, he dug out the young trees and put them in holes out in the lawn, where they could thrive. He might as well have sentenced them to death.

It was the first week of July with deep heat. These trees were in the full thrust of the growing season. Much of their fluid, and energy, was in their green leaves. They were adapted to shade. Within hours, the strong sunlight burned their tender leaves. The yanked roots, even well watered, couldn't supply enough water to the leaves. The trees went into shock. Leaves crumpled and fell. The plants could not survive.

Alas, midsummer is when lots of us have ideas. We sit in lawn chairs, or lie in hammocks, or peek out windows, and see plants in full flower. We brainstorm about moving trees and rearranging plants. But it's not time to do this work. Ambitions must wait.

Early spring, fall, or winter are much better for transplanting—especially for trees and shrubs. At those times of year, the sunshine and heat are not as intense, so a plant doesn't easily dry out and go into shock. The plant isn't vigorously growing, hasn't put all its energy into its far reaches, its leaves and shoots. The fluids and energy are still in the roots and main stems. So it can adjust to a move.

In our area, an ideal time for tree planting is fall, a month before the ground freezes. Deciduous trees, which drop leaves, have done so. They don't have leaves to keep up. They are settling in for quiet, deeper growth.

Allowing the Struggle

Who should do the moving of plants? For some transplanting, an adult is needed. But if you have a child who has gardening interest, and a bit of strength, let him or her do the job, if the plant isn't a cherished, expensive one.

Moving plants teaches. Some plants let go easily. Others have roots that are deep, or extensive, or wide. Some plants cannot be pulled from one direction but will let go from another. They must be eased, or rocked, or slowly chopped. Moving a plant is an experience. It teaches about force. It teaches about action, reaction, push, and pull, and effort. (Physics!) It's one of those things where it might be wise to let slightly older kids struggle—alone, or at least with parents at a safe distance. Perhaps pretend to be unavailable even if you are available.

Many gardening lessons are best learned and remembered by experiencing frustration and making mistakes. There is the sadness of killing a plant you were trying to save. (This happens with plants such as butterfly milkweed, which has a taproot and is notoriously hard to transplant.) And there is that satisfaction of succeeding in a task that seemed too great. That's a lot of what gardening is.

21 : NATIVE PLANTS

Whenever you can, choose native plants for your wildlife garden. Native plants are the naturally occurring, indigenous plants of a region. That makes them more likely to benefit local animals, because the relationships among local plants and animals have developed over tens of thousands of years, if not longer. The insects, birds, and mammals that live nearby have the proper digestive systems and behaviors to use these plants for food and shelter.

Native plants are also adapted to local soils and climates. Once established, many are tough and enduring—likely to survive weather extremes such as early freezes, droughts, or heavy rains. So you, as the gardener, don't have to "baby" them as you would a tropical plant in a northern climate or a forest plant in a desert. Many a time, our native savanna and prairie plants have survived long periods with no irrigation, while lawns and flower beds of imported plants died off or only survived because of heavy watering.

Pioneering Plants and Invasives

Native plants also help avoid the problem of invasive species. Over time, people have brought many beloved plants and animals from their homelands to new places. Plants and animals have also hitched rides in and on ships, crates, cars, boot soles, firewood, mulch bags, and Christmas trees. These so-called exotic species arrived in areas where they were not native. Some of these plants and animals settled in, benefited people, and did not cause much issue to local plants and animals. But other exotic plants and animals spread so quickly and widely that they choked out native species. These plants and animals are called "invasives."

Evidently, the predators, parasites, or environmental conditions that limited their populations in their homelands did not exist in their new home. So these plants and animals actually succeeded a bit too well. Garlic mustard and Japanese honeysuckle are crowding out native forest wildflowers in the northeastern and midwestern United States. Reed canary grass is pushing out native grasses from roadsides. Multiflora rose and autumn olive, once recommended as optimal wildlife foods, have become pest species, choking out the native plants in parks. Purple loosestrife, with its beautiful blooms and vigorous roots, has pushed many native plants out of wetlands.

Exotic animals, too, are becoming a problem in some areas. Asian silver carp have overrun the Illinois River, wiping out most of the native fish population. Burmese pythons have become established in the Everglades. Released pets such as guppies and goldfish cause this kind of damage all over the world. Monitor lizards, parrots, and all kinds of exotic creatures can survive the mild winters of Florida, making that state particularly vulnerable to invasive species.

A Practical Approach to Native Plants

Although native plants are a good choice, don't let the search for natives stop you from planting. Sometimes you'll have to compromise with a similar cultivar—a related but non-native variety. Do educate yourself about which plants are invasive in your area, so you don't use them. (Surprisingly, some plant nurseries still sell invasive plants that you really don't want to establish or spread in your yard.) Again, as with so many aspects of wildlife gardening, the issues are highly localized. Non-native butterfly bush and bronzen fennel, which are terrific wildlife choices in our northern Midwest garden, are a disaster in southern California, where these plants take over the landscape. So think carefully before transporting any plants from far distances to your home. State native-plant societies are a good source of information about what plants are native or invasive where you live.

You may have to make some compromises in restoring your land. If your neighborhood was once a wetland or forest, you should try some wetland or forest species. But also consider the current state of your soil and climate. If you live in what was once a wetland, but it no longer has much water, then it's kind of pointless to plant wetland plants. If what the developers did was fill the land by dumping piles of sand from a sand dune, for instance, you may do well with some sandy dune species instead. As with all gardening, experiment.

Getting to Know Your Native Land

Finding and growing your first native plants is a joyful celebration of connection to the land. For many, it feels like reclaiming a piece of Earth. It only takes setting out a few plants to experience this feeling.

Around where we live, folks smile over red columbine, gush about cup plants, and beam when they talk about growing echinacea (purple coneflower) because of all its connections to native medicines and the land. One benefit of native plants, such as prairie plants, is that some have deep roots that develop soil and clean the water that runs off from lawns and streets. (As much as 70 percent of the prairie's plant material is below ground, as roots, not above.) Native plants are being used to filter pollutants out of water from lawn and road runoff, and even in septic systems.

To explore native plants in your region, check to see if you have a local native-plant nursery or state native-plant society. Quite a few botanical gardens have a native-plant garden and conduct yearly native-plant sales. The Lady Bird Johnson Wildflower Center at the University of Texas in Austin, for instance, has extensive exhibits and seeds for sale; it's a first stop for Texas-native plants. The center has led efforts to plant natives on roadsides nationwide.

For a plant to be non-native, it doesn't need to come from another country or continent. A California plant is unlikely to be native to Iowa. A plant from two hundred miles away might be non-native to your particular county. Wildlife managers try to find plants that are as native as possible, from nurseries within their region, so that the seed is adapted to their particular soils and climate. The closer to home a plant was grown, the better chance it has of being adapted to your soils and climate. So purchase from native nurseries that are as close to you as possible.

Talk with a local naturalist, ecological consultant, or native-plants expert. For a fee, perhaps they will walk your property to point out what species you already have and give you suggestions for excellent local additions. If they don't depend on this work for a living, perhaps they will barter services, or share time in exchange for a yummy dinner certificate or a home-cooked meal. If someone is tearing up a piece of land for construction and that land has native plants, get permission to dig a few for your yard. (Don't take plants from wild areas.)

Extend your study by visiting a museum that has exhibits that relate to history and culture. Sites such as Jamestown, in Virginia, have signs and information related to native plants and their uses. If you are fortunate enough to have local people who still preserve traditional ways of gardening with local plants, take their classes and seek their guidance, as well. Let gardening re-root you and your family, connecting you to the native traditions, people, and history of the region where you live.

22 : CACTI FOR WILDLIFE

Newcomers to western desert states may be tempted to plant what they know—often, lush eastern plants and trees. But the southwestern United States has its own palette of beautiful native plants. Arizona, New Mexico, and southern California are studded with mountains that have varying conditions from valley to mountain peak. From baking hot deserts in valleys to cool coniferous forests on mountainsides, the local climate conditions require different kinds of plants. These plants will provide for the local animals and be able to endure the hot, cold, and dry conditions of the West.

For gardeners in desert areas, cactus, for wildlife, is key. Once established, cacti don't need much water to stay healthy. Desert plants have thick stems and leaves for storing water. Agave and cacti plump with moisture after desert rains. As water is

depleted, agave and other succulents shrink. Other plants, such as ocotillos, sprout new leaves after rain but drop them as conditions dry. Waxy leaves help many desert plants keep water in.

Cacti give animals shade during hot days and shelter during cool nights. Ocotillos produce spectacular red blooms that attract hummingbirds. A bite of cactus provides moisture to a thirsty desert lizard. Prickly pear, fruiting, is a wildlife buffet. Flickers, cactus wrens, quail, verdins, thrashers, squirrels, tortoises, and lizards show up to eat prickly pear fruit.

Agave, with its pointed leaves and airy structure, adds structural interest to a garden, plus it creates a spot for hummingbird or oriole nests. Flycatchers and woodpeckers use agave as hunting perches and nesting sites. Cactus wrens nest among the spines of jumping cholla cactus.

Part of childhood learning in the desert is the experience of getting pricked by cactus. It's unavoidable, really. It's one of those painful lessons about watching where you put your hands and feet. (Adult newcomers to the desert learn this one, too!) Still, while designing exploration spaces for kids, it does make sense to keep jumping cholla a bit back from play areas so no one bumbles into one when diving for a football or a Frisbee.

Desert Blooms

The date you can expect to see blooms on cacti and desert trees will vary. Cacti in the southwestern United

States bloom anywhere from February to November. It depends on the plant species. Native wildflowers—the annual ones that sprout, grow, bloom, then set seed in just a few weeks—are heavily dependent on the timing of seasonal rains. Flowering sometime between February and April is common. A few bloom between July and October. Information sites such as www.desertusa.com and www.dbg.org gather reports and photos of the wildflower blooms during the desert wildflower season.

Where to Buy

Buying specimens from a reputable plant dealer is crucial. "Cacti rustlers" sometimes steal cacti from parks and private lands in order to resell them. Your best bet is to contact a native-plant society, a botanical garden, or a state's cooperative extension service. These organizations can direct you to commercial nurseries or seed companies that are reputable. Also, these organizations often have native-plant sales. For example, the Arizona Game and Fish Department's website, www.azgfd.gov, has publications about wildlife gardening.

Grouping Plants

To provide maximum shelter for wildlife, group some of your cacti together. A spiny mesh of crisscrossed cacti is a good retreat for lizards escaping cats and dogs. Rocks and log piles add to the habitat for creatures such as ornate tree lizards, regal horned lizards, and tiger whiptails. (For more advice on encouraging lizards in the Southwest, see the Arizona Native Plant Society brochure "Where Do Lizards Lounge?" available at www.aznps.com/documents/lizardbrochure.2.pdf.)

Planting a Desert-Annual Wildflower Garden

Have a spot in a dry, desert garden? Plant annual desert wildflowers. The Phoenix Desert Botanical Garden recommends October, November, and December as good months for plantings. Plenty of sun and good drainage are necessary for these kinds of annual flowers.

Don't bury the seeds of desert annuals, as you would seeds in many other habitats. Scatter the seeds atop the soil. Moisten the area and keep it moist until the seeds have sprouted and the seedlings have taken hold. Then water as needed. Take your cue from the plants. If they are wilted, water them. Enjoy the view.

Like all annuals, these plants, if allowed to flower and form seed, will come back. But desert wildflower seeds can lie dormant for years. The next bout of rains may bring forth your wildflower garden. Of course, if water is available, you can water them and see the plants sprout and grow. For a list of desert wildflowers, check with a desert botanical garden such as the Arizona—Sonora Desert Museum in Tucson or the Phoenix Desert Botanical Garden. They have pamphlets, website sources, and, of course, exhibits. A good book for further reading is *Landscaping with Native Plants of the Southwest* by George Oxford Miller.

23 : PLANTING THE GREAT ONES

When I drive through many tree-shaded neighborhoods in our town, I see beauty but lack of planning: all the trees are the same age. Stately trees, widely spaced, and lawns are the norm. "Wooded Estates" reads the sign. Yet after a tornado, or even after simple storms, this neighborhood will not be wooded at all. No one is getting a head start, thinking about the next generation of trees. As much as we might wish it, replacing a one-hundred-year old tree with a tiny seedling is not the same thing. Losing that full-grown tree is the loss of perhaps a quarter acre of habitat surface.

A neighborhood of only older trees is like a neighborhood with no children. What will the future hold for families, for squirrels, for birds? Who will speak for them and the trees they will need? Start now. Time makes a difference. Each tree you plant and

maintain will change the world for wildlife and future children.

Which Trees Are Best?

Every tree is an addition to the wildlife habitat. But certain trees stand above all. These are the great ones—the long-lived, stately trees that shape a neighborhood. Many are slow growers, but they give the biggest payoff to family and to future. In our area of the country, the stately ones are oaks, hickories, maples, beeches, and sycamores. American beech trees, in particular, grow slowly, while sycamores, if their roots reach a significant water source, can shoot up to forty feet tall in just a decade.

Planting smaller trees such as redbuds, dogwoods, or pear trees isn't as much of a commitment. They give a quick payoff and aren't such a problem with power lines. But planting the "great ones" gives the satisfaction of returning to an old neighborhood and finding a tree you planted has grown stately—and that's something that should not be missed by anyone.

Obtaining Trees for Planting

Where should you obtain trees for planting? Often, a first instinct is to transplant small, spare trees from other places. But transplanting wild trees has a low success rate. Many species, such as oaks, put their first energy into a deep taproot that is easy to break during transplanting. If you're hoping to move trees this way, your best bet is to move several and hope one survives.

Purchasing a potted tree or tree in burlap covering from a nursery provides a better chance of success, because the tree will not be in as much shock from being transplanted, roots broken.

Free or inexpensive trees can sometimes be obtained from the Natural Resources Conservation Service (formerly called the Soil Conservation Service), a state forestry service, or conservation organizations such as Arbor Day (www.arborday.org). A native-plant nursery or native-plant sale will offer species most suitable to your habitat and the native creatures. In many regions, native-tree nurseries specialize in growing bare-root or potted native trees and shrubs. The expertise of these horticulturalists allows them to properly grow and prepare bare root stock.

Letting the Trees Grow

If your habitat is a wooded area or near a wooded area, you may not need to plant trees at all. The key may be to let planted trees grow. Keep an eye out for saplings (small, young trees) that sprout up in the lawn or flower beds. Squirrels and jays in the area may have already planted oaks and hickories. They "cache," or store the nuts in the ground, but return to eat only some of them. Some sprout and grow. If you are fortunate enough to have these tree planters, just decide which saplings to keep. Mark off an area around the tree you are keeping, so it won't be pulled or mowed. Or transplant these very young trees, if they have not sent down a deep taproot.

Effective Tree Planting

The best times for planting are the quiet times: quiet times for plants. These are the seasons when plants are not stressed by extremely hot, cold, windy, or dry weather. When that season is, of course, depends on where you live. In the midwestern and northeastern United States, that time is spring or fall. A plant without leaves can focus its energy on roots and getting established, which is the most important role for a tree in a new place.

Also important in tree planting is digging a hole big enough for the tree roots. A tree needs space to spread out. If the soil around the site is compacted, due to hard clay, for instance, you can help the tree by digging widely, creating a space for its roots. Folding up the tree's roots is counterproductive. If you purchase a tree in a pot, remove the pot and gently loosen any roots that are compressed and winding around just below the pot's plastic. This will help them grow outward, into the soil.

Don't bury the tree too deeply. The tree should be planted at the same level in the ground that it was in the nursery. Look at the base of the tree for soil and water marks to help indicate the level to which the tree was buried.

25 : GIVING TREES
SPACE TO GROW

The roots of trees need a lot more space than most people realize. Look at the crown (the spread-out branches) of the top of the tree. Then look down at the ground. As a general rule, trees' roots take up as much space as their crown. So a tree with a trunk that is a foot wide doesn't just need a few more feet of space around it: it may, in fact, need to draw from roots that spread ten or twenty feet out from the trunk.

Of course, there is variation. Some species of trees rely heavily on a taproot, which pushes deep into the ground and "taps" into groundwater. Other trees rely more on a wide, spread-out network of small roots that draw from water sources near the surface.

Many trees pull from a combination of a taproot and a wide network of roots. The point is, just as the smaller plants in your garden need plenty of space to grow, a tree needs plenty of space for its branches and roots to spread. Make sure you provide that space when you first plant it, but also consider its needs as it grows taller and older. A tree's feet—its roots—need respect.

Tree Circles

Find a place with some sizable trees—a foot or more in diameter. This might be in your yard or in a park, university grounds, or botanical garden. Take your kids on a trip of imagining. Have them look at a tree. From far away. From close up. Have them stretch out their arms, like the branches of a tree. Have them walk a circle around the tree to indicate how far they think its roots reach outward.

Then have them look more closely. Can they see signs of the trees' roots where roots poke up out of the soil? Have them walk a new circle. They make this circle by looking up at the tree's crown. Now they can imagine how far the roots probably reach outward. Have them repeat their root circles for other trees, as well.

Respecting the Feet of the Trees

How does one respect the feet of the trees? Trees need water. So they need as much unpaved space around them as possible. If the area needs pathways, then build them of gravel, wood chips, or other porous materials through which water can reach the trees' roots.

Also hugely important is compaction—or lack thereof. Tree roots and the fungi that help tree roots absorb nutrients need air spaces in the soil. Through these spaces creatures crawl, air flows, and water seeps. It is essential. Construction machinery—any heavy machine—going over and over the soil can squash out the air. For a small tree, even people walking back and forth right beside it can compact the soil and make it difficult for water to seep in. Rarely, too, the opposite occurs. The soil may be too loose, without enough compaction to hold the tree in place.

Tree Bark Care

Protect the trees in your wildlife habitat by installing rocks, edging, or other barriers that keep mowers and Weedwackers from passing too close to trees. Many urban trees die from being repeatedly bumped or cut by yard maintenance machines.

Water and nutrients flow up trees through their xylem and phloem, which are right underneath the outer bark. Cutting this layer interrupts the flow of these nutrients. Insects and diseases also enter holes in trees. So cutting initials into trees not only defaces their natural beauty—it can, over time, weaken the trees.

You may also need to wrap the trunks of smaller trees to keep deer from nibbling them. Just be sure to wrap them with material that leaves plenty of room for tree growth and does not trap moisture against the trunk, leading to rot.

25 : CELEBRATING SNAGS

Pink with flowers in spring, green with heart-shaped leaves in summer, our redbud tree was a beauty. Then it died. Fortunately, we were not very quick to clean up things. We left the "dead" tree standing. That's when we discovered its ongoing value.

Birds lined up in the tree before flying to the feeder. So we called it the "queue tree." (Lining up is called "queueing" in Britain.) Even better, the bare tree gave us a view of the birds—no leaves or flowers in the way. That was perfect for us, as wildlife photographers.

Months later, another surprise came our way. The tree resprouted from its trunk and a full tree soon grew out of the trunk alongside the dead form. Eventually that dead form fell. This dying and sprouting has happened several times over the last fifteen years. At times, it pays to delay clean up. Wait and see what a tree—or mess—might have in store. In the temperate rain forests of the Pacific Northwest United States, fallen trees act as "nurse logs," helping produce and shelter trees to come. (In other forests, these fallen trees shelter seedlings, as well.) In nature, what an outsider labels "waste" may very well be an important ingredient in renewal to come.

Dead trees that are still standing—called "snags"—are some of the most valuable trees for wildlife. Broken-off branches and jagged ends provide wildlife perches and woodpecker drilling sites. As the snag rots, its softened wood becomes easier for birds to drill for insects and excavate for homes. Raccoons, possums, and flying squirrels move into hollow branches. A snag is a wildlife haven.

Some people believe that a tree, once it dies, will immediately become weak and fall. That's not the case. Trees, living and dead, often hollow out as their heartwood rots. Yet even a hollow tree can stand for many years. A hollow cylinder is quite a stable structure. That's why it's often used in construction; it's strong yet uses minimal materials.

A dead tree that drops its leaves is more streamlined than a living tree. If hollow, it supports less weight. So a snag can often endure a bit more wind than some living trees weighed down by rain-soaked or ice-covered leaves.

In this part of its life cycle, the snag is an apartment building for wildlife—owls, raccoons, and other creatures. So even if you have to cut an overhanging branch off a snag, consider leaving part of its trunk standing, if safely possible. Even a snag that's eight feet tall can have some value for wildlife. The snag will be a birdhouse you don't have to build. Or, if you have plenty of bird nesting sites, plant flowering vines at its base and you'll have a beautiful natural trellis and wildlife perch. Perhaps a great blue heron will land on it. Or a raccoon will stretch out, atop it, in the sun. Snags pay off, tremendously, in wildlife sightings.

Creating a Queue Tree

Sometimes a tree is in the wrong place for your yard. A tree seedling sprouts, and gets away from you—and perhaps it grows many feet tall before you get around to

weeding it from a bed. By then its roots are deep and strong. Perhaps it begins to shade or draw nutrients from a desirable garden area. One solution is to cut it down. But why not make it into a queue tree, instead? It can be a perch for birds, a lookout spot for chipmunks, a lattice for vines to climb. It's a free, nature-made sculpture. It's a display shelf not for knickknacks but for colorful birds and dragonflies.

If the tree has not died on its own, you can help it along. You can kill most trees by girdling them. Using a handsaw or saw pruner, you simply cut into the tree just a little bit, all the way around the trunk. Make a circle, like a girdle. You should be cutting the bark and a bit of the layer underneath. (Obviously, don't cut so much that the tree falls down.) Leave the tree, and over several weeks, the leaves will die and drop. (What happens depends on the tree species. Some, such as sumacs, will resprout.)

Now enjoy your queue tree. Sketch it, learn it, draw it. Name it. Have your kids observe what creatures make use of it. You may even want to decorate it for the holidays with some wildlife treats—corn, oranges, small bags of seeds—and other wild animal foods.

26 : WATER GARDENING

When Jeff said, "How about we put in a water garden?" I was thinking a water garden meant a half a barrel, some water lilies, and a couple of fish. Well, three years and four tons of stone later, our three-pool water garden, complete with a raceway, bog, and waterfall, was done. Almost every family member and friend had been pulled into the grand production. There'd been a couple years of me staring doubtfully at massive holes filled with rubber and rocks. But, oh, the results! Water striders, dragonflies, frogs, and turtles became part of our lives, and the comforting bubbling sound of the water garden became a focal point of our yard. You don't have to "dig in" with such a big plan. But I recommend a water garden. Even a small one will help wildlife and bring new adventures and new creatures to your life.

Water Garden 101

The basics of a water garden are simple. You dig a hole and line it with some material that will keep the water from percolating down into the soil. On top of that liner you add at least a few rocks. These help secure the liner and create crevices where creatures can shelter and aquatic plants can root. Fill the lined hole with water. Install some kind of a dripper or water pump to circulate the water and keep it free of mosquitoes. Every now and then, add more water because some will evaporate if you don't get enough rain.

Building a water garden can be a free-form, small-scale project. Or it can be a big production with technical specifications and plans. Companies such as Aquascape have catalogs of materials and trained people who help build wildlife pools in case you're doing a big project and don't want to muddle through it, over three years, as we did. How you accomplish each step will determine the scale of your project and how long your water garden lasts. Here are some things to think about for the materials.

The Hole

Water gardens don't need to be deep unless you're wanting fish and turtles to overwinter deep in muck. (The water garden pump should keep the water garden from freezing fully in winter.) A water garden with a variety of depths is optimal because it will suit multiple

creatures. On the other hand, when asked what he'd tell people who are building water gardens, my husband said, "Um, dig a bigger hole than you think you'll need!" Once you add the liner, rocks, and plants, it's shallower than you might anticipate. Of course, be very careful about safety with hole digging, as digging down in sandy or soft dirt can create unstable sides to a hole, and those sides can suddenly, and dangerously, collapse when digging. Big-hole-digging is not a one-person job.

The Liner

A pool liner needs to be made of fish-safe rubber, so toxic materials from the rubber won't poison wildlife. Investing in a good, durable liner will make your pond last longer and prevent frustrating leaks. Before installing the rubber liner, a felt underlayment is usually put down. This helps smooth out the ground and protect the rubber liner from sticks, rocks, and other objects that could puncture the liner from below. An old carpet can also be used for this purpose.

The Rocks

A variety of rock sizes will provide an assortment of surfaces for creatures. Covering liner edges with rocks helps hide the rubber or plastic so it looks better. But you don't have to cover every inch of liner with rock because silt, plants, and other gunk will eventually cover it up, and much of the liner won't be visible from the surface.

The Pump

The water pump needs to be the proper size for the amount of water circulating and the level of the waterfall if you are pumping it uphill. Companies that sell these have charts to calculate which pump is suitable.

The Water

City water has been chlorinated. When you are first filling a water garden, let the water sit before adding any creatures. Later, adding a bit of water, straight from the hose, is not such a big deal. Or, you could let it sit in a bucket so some of the water-cleaning chemicals evaporate before you add it to the pool.

Picking Plants

After building your water garden, you can tuck plants directly into spaces between rocks. Or you can sink a pot of plants right into the water. Try not to be tempted by exotic plants sold by water garden companies and typical plant nurseries. First check with a native-plant nursery and consider using native aquatic and wetland plants. Native plants should have the most benefit for wild creatures. (We had pickerel weed, native white water lily, marsh marigold, arrowhead, blue flag iris, swamp milkweed, blue lobelia, and water plantain.)

As it was elsewhere in your yard, layers are useful in a water garden. This can be accomplished by building a pond with varying depths. Some plants float directly in water. Others live in shallows, with roots underwater but a lot of their plant material above water. Consider these depths when planting. Each layer adds more places for wild creatures to establish themselves in your pond.

Fish or No Fish

Companies that build water gardens are great resources for dealing with the technical aspects of building water gardens, but they rarely fit their plans and designs to local wildlife. (They sell exotic plants and animals nationwide.) As a wildlife gardener, you'll need to put in some extra research and care to make it fit your habitat.

For instance, think seriously about whether or not you want fish. Fish are fun, but there is a trade-off. Fish make water gardens, especially small ones, less helpful to frogs and dragonflies. Fish eat most of the eggs. Larger fish may eat small turtles. If you love wild, native elements of nature, you may have much more fun just seeing what shows up to colonize your water garden. Water striders will probably show up. Then water boatman and other nifty water insects will arrive. Frogs and water turtles will likely show up if there are any streams or forests nearby. You'll be surprised at how far the creatures will travel. If you are building a water garden with several pools, and you have your heart set on having fish, perhaps put fish only in the lowest pool and leave the others for frogs and dragonflies.

You should think big, and long term, with your water garden or homemade pond. Could a major flood carry those goldfish and other non-native fish into a stream or river near your house? You might be creating a disaster for the native fish if they do. Do not put goldfish and other non-native fish in a water garden close to a natural stream, pond, or river. Keep these fish in a fish tank, indoors, for fishy fun.

Water Filter Fun

If you set up a water garden with a pump, you'll soon be involved with filters. Water flows through mats and baskets before going into the pump. This helps keep plants, tadpoles, turtles, and frogs from getting into the water pump. What seems like it could be a chore—picking plants and critters out of the filters—becomes the big fun of a water garden. Once you see the underwater creatures, you and your kids will want to learn about what they are. With a water garden, hands-on science abounds. Perhaps you'll find a dragonfly just emerging as you open the filter case; help it crawl up on your finger and take it out to settle on a hanging plant so its wings can dry. (Cleaning out the water filter got me so curious about aquatic insects that I ended up writing a related book, *Trout Are Made of Trees!*) To find out what creatures are in your water filter, look for guides to aquatic insects and books related to vernal pools (seasonal pools) and wetlands.

27 : MOWING FOR WILDLIFE

There's a place in a wildlife garden for a bit of short grass. American robins and northern flickers probe lawns for earthworms. Bluebirds swoop for insects. Chipmunks, fox squirrels, and woodchucks dine on mushrooms and bury acorns. It's also useful for kids to have a clear lawn for outdoor games. Lawn may not seem like a natural habitat. Certainly, pesticide-covered lawns or those planted with a single species of grass are not. Yet areas of short, close-clipped grass existed before people came to North America. The mowers, back then, were bison!

So go ahead, mow a little, if you like. We've reduced our lawn to an area small enough to mow with a battery-powered electric mower. This is great for us, because it's quiet and doesn't give off the exhaust that irritates our asthma. Many gasoline-powered

mowers put out as much pollution as a small car. Friends of ours go even more minimal, with a human-powered push mower.

Walking mowers give one a chance to look more closely and stop if a toad or some other creature is in the mower's path. It's not pleasant to think of the insects that are inadvertently killed by mowing. But after mowing, the sliced up insects and scared up insects attract insect-eating birds to the lawn.

Country Acres

What if you live in the country and have quite a bit of land? For the best results, consult an expert naturalist or local ecological consulting firm about how to manage these larger properties for wildlife. Don't assume a forest will be the best boon for wildlife. Birds need natural grasslands, too. In fact, grassland birds are some of the most endangered.

Meadowlarks, field sparrows, and bobolinks fill grasslands with beautiful melodies. Natural grasslands have medium-height to tall grasses with deep, soil-producing roots. Native grasses are best. A native grassland can help rare birds such as grasshopper sparrows and upland sandpipers survive. (Unfortunately, many fields have been planted with non-native grasses that look similar to the natural habitat but do not provide food in the seasons the animals need them.)

Fire can be part of the natural cycle of nature in grasslands. Some plants need fire to open their seed pods and ash to fertilize the ground where they will grow. Fire also suppresses other plants that might outcompete these fire-adapted species. Grassland fires move incredibly quickly, so controlled burns need a skilled, trained crew.

You may be able to mow or harvest some of the grasses for hay. But burning should be done before grassland birds arrive in spring. Quite a few grassland bird species nest on the ground, or directly in grasses, not in nearby trees. So leaving the grasses undisturbed during nesting season is crucial. Talk with your local Audubon folks about when the grassland birds of your region fledge—leave their nests. Mowing or burning can also be done in the fall, after chicks have fledged. With good maintenance, if you're lucky, you may host fascinating creatures such as woodcocks, which use pencil-like bills to probe the ground for earthworms. Woodcocks favor low to medium-height grass fields for their spiraling courtship displays.

28 : WHEN A FENCE IS MORE THAN A FENCE

The flower garden in front of my office was being eaten by rabbits. So I installed a small fence—a bit of wire hardware cloth just a couple of feet tall. This barrier kept the bunnies out. But as weeks passed, I saw its effects on other species, as well. A toad was trapped inside. Chipmunks, their path blocked, ran alongside it. Songbirds no longer had a direct route to swoop into the bushes, so they didn't hop in view of my window as often. A hunting hawk hopped into the fenced area and chased a songbird, trapping it inside the fencing. I was surprised by how my small fence impacted the animals that used the yard.

On a bigger scale, fencing certainly changes life for wildlife. In the western United

States, fencing is a huge problem for pronghorn, America's fleet-footed, gazelle-like mammal. Because the migrating animals won't leap over the fences, they die against them, or get tangled in them, as they try to migrate to winter and summer feeding grounds. The National Parks Conservation Association and other people who care about pronghorns are asking landowners to change their fencing. If the lowest wire is at least eighteen inches off the ground, the pronghorns can crawl under it, while most cattle stay in. So with a change in fencing, some landowners are helping pronghorn survive.

Fencing for Mammals in an Urban Environment

When we moved into our present home, it already had a large fenced backyard area for a dog. Even though we do not have a dog, we left the fence anyway. With the addition of wildlife plantings, the yard became a mammal haven. Why? Because animals could feed undisturbed by dogs, which are frequently off leashes and dashing around the neighborhood. Behind our house, squirrels, skunks, raccoons, and even an occasional fox or possum could wander and feed in peace.

Consider the pros and cons of fencing in your yard. What you have learned about animals' movements through your yard, from earlier chapters and studies, can help you decide if a fence will help or hinder the wildlife you want to attract. The type of fencing, of course, is crucial, too. The sizes of slats, spaces between wires or boards, and height of the fence will all impact creatures, keeping them in or out.

29 : KEEPING THE NEIGHBORS HAPPY

Up to now, we've only talked about keeping the wild neighbors happy. But human neighbors have needs and opinions, too. The degree to which your wildlife garden needs to be manicured depends on where you live and the rules and standards in your community. If you live within city limits, there may be weed ordinances on the heights of grass. Usually these aren't enforced unless a neighbor complains. Alas, to the untrained eye, a garden that is left to brown and provide seed and shelter for small animals just looks like dead or messy stuff.

Here are some ways to help your garden fit into the neighborhood. (I confess we personally haven't done a great job at that; we live in the county, and the views and standards are more flexible than within the city limits.)

Borders

Have distinctive tamed areas and wild areas. A cleanly
kept edging of rocks, a low wall, or a split-rail fence gives
people who are freaked out by wild areas some sense
that they are "in control." If you have a forest area with
plenty of undergrowth, mow a small border, a few feet
wide, near the road edge so that it's obvious that your
wild area is intentional, and not just neglected. Pathways,
too, make it seem more "tame" to many. This mowing
project is also a good responsibility for growing teens.

Showy Flowers

Give your neighbors some seasonal joy by planting a
few tamer flower beds, flowering trees, and perennial
beds near the road. Throw in a few recognizable species
that flower lovers might like. We have gobs of daffodils
and other bulbs in those front beds. It's a way to distract
neighbors' attention from the rest of the chaos, which to
us is biodiversity but to them is more of a jungly secret
garden. Redbud trees and dogwoods put on a show every
year.

Screens

Plant a natural screen. I have yet to meet a person who
does not smile when seeing sunflowers. A tall row of
them adds fun and blocks other views. Native sunflower-
like species such as cup plants are even better. They

return year after year without the need for replanting. We use a long swath of them to curtain our next-door neighbor's driveway from ours.

Share the Garden

The best thing you can do is to invite neighbors in. Have a tea party. Share extra plants, in pots, at the end of your drive. Offer to plant or to help others. Have your children create a StoryWalk™ for the neighborhood, in which they take apart a book, laminate it, and make signs along a walking path. (For information on how this is being done in parks and communities nationwide, check www.kellogghubbard.org/storywalk.) Perhaps your kids can create an event for local kids, in your yard, as well. A yearly tour or fun event can make what you are doing with landscaping understandable and welcomed. Most of what needs to be done is to change the eyes and hearts of people who see nature landscaping. See chapter 52 to learn about certifying your wildlife garden and putting up permanent signs to share your accomplishments with neighbors walking past who may be wondering about what you're up to. Offer to help plant a butterfly garden for someone else, as well. Help nature take hold.

Part Three

WELCOMING BUTTERFLIES, BEES, BATS, DRAGONFLIES, AND TOADS

Do you have a butterfly child—a girl or boy who is charmed by butterflies? (Or a butterfly grown-up? Butterfly fascination knows no age!) If so, then this section is for you.

Late one August afternoon, a question mark butterfly landed on my hat, then my arm, then my hand. A dozen times. The experience seemed spiritual, almost magical. Yet I was curious about the science behind it. Could I encourage butterflies to land more frequently?

I experimented with various locations, clothes, and behaviors. What I learned helped me repeat that butterfly encounter experience and can help you increase your family's chances of beautiful butterfly encounters, too. In case you're wondering, actively pursuing butterfly encounters, even knowing more about the science behind them, doesn't diminish their power at all. The thrill of butterfly landings continues. With a little work, you can invite butterflies, dragonflies, native bees, bats, and toads to your wildlife habitat as well.

30 : BUTTERFLY SEEKERS

One of the first steps to encountering butterflies is knowing them. Seek out a field guide to butterflies in your area. (My all-time favorite butterfly-learning books are *The Family Butterfly Book* by Rick Mikula and *Butterflies through Binoculars* by Jeffrey Glassberg, but there are plenty of other books, too.) Each type of butterfly has a different kind of behavior, so reading about butterfly species in your area can really pay off. In the Midwest, where I live, question marks seem the most likely to land on people. Many species of blues, which flutter near streams in forests, land on people, too. Experiment and find out what works in your area.

When seeking out butterflies in your yard, a local park, or any natural habitat, start with these butterfly-beckoning behaviors:

SEARCH WHEN BUTTERFLIES ARE ACTIVE. Butterflies are not active at night. So it's no use looking for them then. (But moth viewing can be fun! Search near lights for these beauties.) Butterflies also hide out during rain. In cool regions, butterflies are usually not active in early morning. Search for them later if air temperatures where you live are chilly. Think warm and sunny if you are a butterfly seeker.

Don't bother looking for butterflies in winter unless you live in Mexico or the southern United States. In wintertime, in cold places, butterflies hide. They overwinter as eggs, caterpillars, chrysalids, or adults. They hide under bark, in log piles, among leaves, even in seedpods. The best butterfly months vary from region to region. A few butterflies, such as the mourning cloak butterfly, flap around on a warm, sunny day even in February in Indiana, where we live. But that's about it until April. Some common summer butterflies here begin life farther south. It is only after they have lived several generations of stages—egg, caterpillar, adult—that they move far enough north for us to see them. Buckeye butterflies show up in May. August is the time when there are the most butterflies in our area. But we see butterflies late in September and even November. Many of the butterflies we see in early to mid-fall are monarchs, traveling southward to Mexico.

SPEND TIME NEAR BUTTERFLY PLANTS. Spending time outside in a place with butterfly plants is the first way to increase your chance of being "landed on." Unlike hummingbirds, butterflies can't hover well. So butterfly plants are ones that have perches. Daisy petals and sunflower petals give butterflies a place to land. Flat-topped clusters of flowers, such as yarrow, are good, too. But butterflies break the rules, at times. They land on spikes of flowers with small petals such as butterfly bush and liatris. Don't forget flowering trees and shrubs; wild cherry trees are a magnet for butterflies. Check with a local nature center, native-plant society, or garden center to find out about butterfly plants in your area. Stroll through an outdoor garden center during butterfly season and see where the butterflies land. The insects will show you what they prefer.

CHECK NEAR PUDDLES. Large numbers of butterflies gather at puddles, stream edges, and wet sand near ponds. Scientists think that the butterflies are licking natural salt left behind as the puddle water dries. So sandy and muddy stream, river, and pond shores are good places to find butterflies. If you are bathing or sunning near a stream, you increase your chances of being landed on. In these environments, they seem to seek out exposed skin. Perhaps you are providing salt, too! They also gather at puddles formed after rain in muddy hiking paths and dirt roads.

CHECK ON HILLTOPS. Certain butterfly species are "hilltoppers," so named because they spend a lot of time in high places such as hilltops. There, male and female butterflies gather. Some flutter and circle, performing butterfly dances, of a sort. Another butterfly attraction, usually harder for butterfly watchers to access, is treetop flowers. A building or tower that looks out among treetops is a great place for butterfly viewing and encounters.

SIT SLIGHTLY ABOVE FLOWERS. Be a hilltop! Some butterflies, such as the question mark, seem to prefer to perch in high places, such as the highest flower in a meadow. Many times butterflies have landed on me when I am sitting in a chair, or on top of a table, in the midst of a patch of flowers. You only need to be a few inches taller than the highest flowers nearby in order to be a good perch.

BE PATIENT. Mostly, it takes patience and quiet to encounter butterflies. Patience can be learned. I shake out my arms and legs before I sit down to be quiet. That helps my muscles to remain still. While I am waiting for butterflies, I breathe deeply. I watch clouds and birds. I sketch in a notebook. Slowly my body and mind quiet

themselves. I listen. I look. Often, when I have almost given up on butterflies, one lands on me.

BUTTERFLY BINOCULARS. People who love butterfly watching sometimes buy "butterfly-watching binoculars." They really do work. These are the same kind of binoculars used to watch birds, but they are capable of focusing at much closer distances. They're also great for dragonfly and frog watching.

VISIT A BUTTERFLY EXHIBIT. Botanical gardens and natural history museums often have live butterfly exhibits—the kind where you walk in large greenhouses where many butterflies are being raised. For example, the Peggy Notebært Nature Museum in Chicago features not only the exotic butterflies imported for use in these exhibits but also solid information about local species and host plants. There you can find out more about butterflies, while enjoying some captive butterfly encounters. Those exhibits have many butterflies in an enclosed space, so butterfly landings can happen more frequently than in most wild situations. (This will provide "butterfly smiles" in chilly seasons and warm you up for butterfly experiences in the wild.)

VISIT A BUTTERFLY MIGRATION HOTSPOT. Another possibility for experiencing butterfly landings, and for butterfly viewing, is to travel to a butterfly migration hotspot, an area where butterflies rest during migration. Point Pelee, a spit of land in Ontario, Canada, that extends into Lake Erie, is one monarch butterfly hotspot. In general, the shores of the Great Lakes are good places to see monarchs. They flutter along the lake shores and avoid the open water as much as possible. Sometimes they concentrate on a tip of land before they fly across a body of water, or after they have crossed one.

PURCHASE CAPTIVE BUTTERFLIES. Some biological supply companies and education supply stores sell butterfly gardens and cages. These are temporary housing for both wild and captive-raised butterflies. The most common species sold is the European painted lady butterfly, *Vanessa cardui*. It is a widespread butterfly, living on five continents, including North America, which is why it can be sold and released at any time of year. (Although it is unlikely to find food plants in some habitats at the times of year it is released in schools.) This painted lady is a different species from the quite similar looking American painted lady butterfly, *Vanessa virginiensis*.

31 : FINDING THE BEST SPOT FOR YOUR BUTTERFLY GARDEN

Building a butterfly garden is the best way to bring butterflies to your area. But if you're intent on butterfly landings, you'll have to do extra advance planning. The key to butterfly landings is location, location, location.

The number-one time when butterflies land on me is in the late afternoon or early evening. There are trees around our yard, and as the sun sets, some of the yard is in shadow while some of it remains sunny. I sit in those sunny areas as they grow smaller and smaller. Butterflies trying to collect their last bit of nectar or display time gather in these last patches of sunlight. I make myself into a convenient perch, so they land on me.

Before you plant a butterfly garden, work with your family to figure out where the spots of sun and shadow are in your yard. Rustle up some site markers from the house. Popsicle sticks, small branches, or ribbons will do. In late afternoon and early evening, you and your children can mark the last area of bright sun in your yard. This will be your butterfly garden plot.

Take into consideration the change of seasons. For instance, if you're planning in spring, consider where the sun will fall in late summer. Keep in mind that the sun's position in the sky changes over the course of the year. In late summer, the sun—relative to our yard—is lower in the sky, so it hides behind trees. The location for your garden may be altered by the way the sun moves in relation to your yard. The butterfly landing garden should stretch over that whole range, if possible. It should be positioned where that patch of light is, late evening, during the most butterfly-active month in your area. For those of us in the upper Midwest, that would be late July and August.

Does all this calculating sound daunting? It doesn't need to be precise. It can also be an opportunity for you and your kids to go hunting for clues. Do you have photos from previous years that show sun and shade spots? Do you remember where you put lawn chairs, or where you sought shade last year? Have fun puzzling it out. If there was ever a time to read some children's books about the sun and sundials, this is it! It may take a refresher course, and some charting, for you to work out the best garden position. And if the figuring gets too tiresome, just dig in and plant. The butterflies won't mind. The point is just to bring them to your area. Butterflies like sunny spots; that's all you need to remember.

Once you've chosen the location for your butterfly garden, it's time to start planting butterfly flowers (see the next chapter for ideas). As you design your garden, be sure to include several perches—tall perches for your kids and you. This way you will all be "hilltops," perches for butterflies to land. Nothing fancy is necessary. A chair, a rock, a bench will do. It depends on the height of the flowers. You just need to be a bit taller than they are.

32 : PLANTS FOR A BUTTERFLY GARDEN

Like bees, butterflies and moths pollinate flowers. Flowers lure butterflies and moths with a sweet reward: nectar. With a proboscis (that curled, tongue-like structure), a butterfly or moth sips nectar from a flower. As an insect moves around a flower, pollen rubs off on its feet and the rest of its body. Then, when it lands on another flower, this pollen falls or rubs off and pollinates that plant's ovaries.

Pollen that lands on a flower of a different species is a waste. It doesn't pollinate. So many plants, over time, have evolved to attract a certain kind of pollinator, such as bees, butterflies, or wasps. This increases the chance they'll receive the right pollen, not

a kind that is useless to them. Some plants have cues—colors, shapes, and patterns—that attract particular species. A few plants have structures, such as long tubes, that hold their nectar where only certain bat, moth, or bird species are likely to reach it.

Flowers with Perches

Butterfly flowers tend to face upward and have perches such as firm, outstretched petals. Daisies, coneflowers, black-eyed Susans, and most daisy-like flowers serve well. Clusters of flowers facing upward and making a flat head, such as yarrow, attract butterflies. Spikes of small flowers, such as liatris, lure them, too. There's no universal color for butterfly flowers; the insects will visit many colors of blooms.

To find out about butterfly plants native to your area, check a local park or botanical garden. The Phoenix Desert Botanical Garden, for example, recommends desert milkweed, desert globe mallow, desert senna, Baja fairy duster, Goodding's verbena, black dalea, Arizona passionflower, and ageratum as good butterfly flowers for desert habitats. Many are on display in their wildlife garden.

Flowers at Many Times

To keep butterflies in your yard as long as possible, put in plants that bloom throughout the summer. Especially helpful are plants that bloom when monarch butterflies are migrating and need fuel for their journey.

Feed the Caterpillars

Caterpillars grow to become butterflies, so consider caterpillar needs in your gardening. Plant host plants—plants that butterflies lay eggs upon and that caterpillars eat as they grow up.

Which plant hosts which butterfly caterpillar? Many field guides to butterflies have an index to host plants in the back of the book. Check for the butterflies you have locally, and you may be able to find out about host plants, too. There are some excellent field guides to caterpillars, such as David Wagner's *Caterpillars of Eastern North America.*

Many small plants that at first seem like weeds popping up in the lawn—plantain, pussytoes, sedges—turn out to be critical host plants for butterflies. Herbs such as parsley can host swallowtail caterpillars. Young native cherry trees are host to tiger swallowtails. Sassafras host the gorgeous, snake-like spicebush swallowtail caterpillars. And the tomato hornworms that eat tomato plants turn into beautiful hovering hawk moths, enough reason to let them eat a few tomato plants along the way.

Milkweeds feed monarch and queen butterflies. Although common milkweed is their best-known host plant, monarchs also lay eggs on a wide variety of other milkweeds, including butterfly milkweed, swamp milkweed, and purple milkweed. Planting host plants helps increase the overall population of butterflies. Having host plants also increases your butterfly viewing immediately, as the egg-laying butterflies will see or smell the host plants and flutter around your habitat to visit them.

Create a Fruitful Butterfly Spot

In the American tropics, wildlife enthusiasts set out fruit for butterflies and fruit-eating birds. (Various opossums and monkeys visit the fruit, too.) Offering fruit is not a common practice in the continental United States, which has a more temperate climate and different butterfly species—still, it's worth a try.

While I was picking blueberries at a farm, a lady at a nearby bush shared that she makes apple butter and cider every year. She puts out the half-rotten mash of apples to attract loads of butterflies. If you're going to try out this butterfly-attraction method, don't do it too close to where kids play, because you're likely to bring in some wasps as well. Put the fruit up high enough so that you enjoy the view but not all the wasp visitors.

Too Many Butterflies

For all of us who thrill to butterfly landings, it's hard to imagine too many butterflies. Yet Texas sometimes has an astounding influx of a species known as snout butterflies. When heavy rains follow a period of drought, the caterpillars fatten up on spiny hackberry plants and, over generations, build up to tremendous numbers and rise to form visible clouds of butterflies in the sky. My husband and I saw the remnants of a snout butterfly outbreak when I was visiting schools in Texas. The insects were numerous in the air around the truck stops, and they smashed on car windows as people drove. Children said that weeks before, when the butterfly outbreak had been at its peak, they had had a hard time playing soccer because they kept getting the butterflies caught in their mouths! Only a few species of butterflies build up to these numbers in the modern age. Most, like monarchs, are in dire need of habitat, especially host plants for the caterpillars. Your wildlife garden can help.

33 : THE CATERPILLAR CRAWL

When people speak of butterfly plants, they're usually talking about what adult butter-flies eat. But what about caterpillars? Host plants, the plants that caterpillars eat, are a magnet for the adult butterflies, as well, because the adult butterflies have to visit these plants to lay their eggs. Well-placed milkweeds, asters, parsley, fennel, wild cherry trees, sedges, and other host plants will help caterpillars and, thus, butterfly generations.

Searching for Caterpillars

How do you know if you've succeeded in encouraging caterpillars to settle in your yard? Take your kids on a caterpillar crawl! No actual crawling necessary. But moving slowly and carefully will help. You can try out this activity any time of year when caterpillars are active. In the Midwest and East, mid- to late summer is a great time for a caterpillar search.

Many caterpillars hide and are well camouflaged. Here in the Midwest, a variety of swallowtail caterpillars mimic the gooey black-and-white droppings of birds. Many other caterpillars look brown like sticks or are green like leaves. So the way to find caterpillars is to look not for them but for their work: partially eaten leaves, droppings, and sleeping roosts.

Partially Eaten Leaves

Search around partially eaten leaves. Be sure to check the undersides of leaves and stems. If the eaten spots of leaves are perfect semicircles and only on leaf edges, they may indicate another amazing creature: the leafcutter bee. Watch the plant to see if a bee visits and cuts leaves.

Caterpillar Droppings

Caterpillar droppings are typically black, gray, or green in color. They can be cylindrical or spherical. The size varies with the caterpillar. But a couple of millimeters long is not uncommon. Finding caterpillar droppings is the main way we locate monarch caterpillars on milkweed.

Caterpillar Roosts

Look for leaves that have rolled-up ends. Don't unroll them. Just peek in the open end. You're likely to find either (1) webbing but no creature, (2) a spider, or (3) a caterpillar. We call these caterpillar "sleeping bags." If you do find a caterpillar, without removing the leaf from the tree, gently open the sleeping roll to peek at the caterpillar. Then close it up and leave it alone. There are several terrific field guides to caterpillars to help identify what you have. Taking a photo on the spot is helpful: even if you think you'll remember exactly how a caterpillar looks, it can be hard to remember a caterpillar's features, such as the number of stripes or arrangement of colors, later on.

34 : DRAGONFLY ENCOUNTERS

Having a dragonfly land on your arm is a breath-catching, slightly nervous joy. Dragonflies don't sting. If handled roughly, they may, in extreme circumstances, pinch. But that is rare. I've had dragonflies land on me dozens of times, and I've handled many while rescuing them from the water-garden skimmer. Yet none has pinched me even in those circumstances.

Seeking Dragonflies

To encourage a dragonfly to land on you, you need to set up the right conditions. Spend time outside near ponds, streams, and meadows where dragonflies are active.

Like butterflies, dragonflies are usually inactive in winter, on rainy days, and on cold early mornings. So late morning through sunset is the best time to encounter them.

If you observe dragonflies, you'll notice that they settle in two main types of places: on thin stems, which give them a view of their territories, and large, light-colored rocks, where they sun themselves. Here are some hints to help encourage dragonfly encounters.

Make Yourself into a Lookout Perch

Sit in a chair near the edge of a pond and prop up your leg. Now your foot will make a good perch, above the other available perches. It doesn't have to be very high. Another trick is to settle near a pond or wetland and hold up a stick as a dragonfly perch. I will tell you from experience that your arm gets very tired from holding up the stick. Sitting with a fishing pole, base propped on the ground, might work better.

Wear Light Clothes and Be a Sunning Spot

Wear white or khaki-colored pants and stretch out a leg so you provide a broad surface, like a sunning rock. Dragonflies may also land on a light-colored shirt, hat, or skirt.

Go Out on Water in a Paddleboat or Canoe

Choose a sunny day when dragonflies are active. Go out on a lake, river, or stream. If you paddle near the water's edge, dragonflies will often land on the boat (or you) to take a rest.

Check the Driveway or Sidewalk

It sounds strange, perhaps, but we sometimes see dragonflies patrolling driveways and sidewalks. Does the shiny surface make the paving seem like a stream? One can only guess!

Check in the Dappled Shade near Wet Areas

The dappled shade near a wet area is a good spot to see damselflies, which are the jewel-winged, slender relatives of dragonflies. Damselflies generally (though not always) keep their wings together when they perch. Dragonflies tend to put their wings out to the side, like biplanes. Damselflies called bluets have clear areas that make watching them a hide-and-seek adventure. In recent years, the appearance of dragonfly and damselfly guide books such as Sidney W. Dunkle's *Dragonflies through Binoculars* have made dragonfly and damselfly identification much simpler.

Sit in the Last Light of the Day

As with butterflies, I've had most of my dragonfly "landings" in the last bit of light of the day. Dragonflies often perch on the sides of houses and sheds to take advantage of the last rays of sun available. You just have to make sure you're sitting in that last patch of sun, and facing the sun. Your shirt and pants should create an expanse where dragonflies might rest and sun themselves. In our area of the country, it's primarily white-tailed dragonflies and widow dragonflies that tend to land on people. Meadowhawks, another kind of dragonfly, perch on plant stems in the garden. Other dragonfly species here in the Midwest are not as active near sunset. You'll find that the dragonfly species in your area vary in their habits, too.

35 : CREATING DRAGONFLY AND DAMSELFLY HABITATS

You can help create habitats for dragonflies and damselflies in backyards, schoolyards, and parks. The first essential is water—flowing water, such as a stream or water garden. Dragonflies need wet areas because for the first few years of their lives, they live as an underwater form called a "nymph." As a dragonfly nymph grows, it sheds its skin several times. Then, during its last molt, it crawls up a stem or rock, splits open its skin, and emerges as a winged adult. Its wings must dry before it is ready to fly. Some dragonflies live several years in their underwater state, then survive only a few weeks as flying adult dragonflies. The transformation of the dragonfly is largely unappreciated, yet it is as spectacular as that of butterflies.

To help in this delicate transition, dragonflies need plants and rocks near wetlands, streams, and ponds. Some dragonflies lay eggs inside or attached to streamside or wetland plant stems. So don't mow right to the edge of wet areas. Get your kids working to encourage neighbors not to mow close to water edges. Plant native plants near these ditches, ponds, and streams, so native creatures can have food and shelter.

Wetland plants such as arrowroot, pickerel weed, white water lily, yellow water lily, water willow, purple iris, riverbank sedge, and mud plantain can also add life and color to a water garden. They can be tucked in between rocks that cover the pond liner. (Mud will sink in, between the roots, as the pond ages.) Plants can also be planted in soil-filled pots and weighed down to stay in the pond. Swamp milkweed and marsh marigold can be planted along the edges. Check with local nature centers, native-plant societies, and naturalists about what suits the water in your area.

Create Dragonfly Sunning Spots and Perches

This is an activity for the youngest nature lovers. Have them search out a few sticks, small branches, or small logs, and put them beside, or partly submerged in, a stream, pond, or water garden. This will provide perches for dragonflies.

Next up, find something light colored, preferably a rock. Don't have a big rock? Think creatively about what wide, broad, light surface might be a good sunning spot for dragonflies. That might be a plastic chair, a wooden bench, a piece of fencing, a wheelbarrow—use your imagination. Have your nature helpers assist you in putting this sunning spot in the last light of the day. It doesn't have to be right beside the water source. In our yard, the rocks and sunning fences where dragonflies spend their last daylight hours are a good fifty yards away from the stream and water garden.

Dragonfly Adventure Outing

To cap your family's study of dragonflies, visit local parks with streams, ponds, and wetlands to find more. Dragonflies tend to migrate along many of the same routes that hawks follow

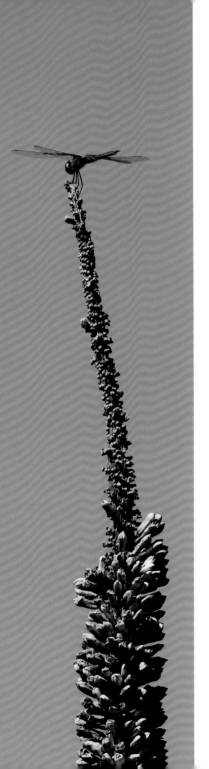

in fall. So research hawk-watching sites, which are usually along lakeshores and mountain ridges. Visit one of these spots and you may find dragonflies as well.

Stream Sampling

If you have a water garden, and have to clean out the skimmer, you'll likely become familiar with dragonfly nymphs, the underwater forms of dragonflies. But there are other ways to see these creatures. Check your area for volunteer stream-sampling projects. To sample, volunteers walk through the stream with a net spread among several people. Then they examine aquatic insects caught in the net. Certain insects live only in very clean water; others predominate where the water is heavily polluted with fertilizers and other pollutants. By looking at the insect species, including dragonfly larvæ, volunteers can monitor the water quality of the stream from year to year. Insect monitoring has proven the success of many stream and river cleaning efforts.

I first learned stream sampling through the Save Our Streams program developed by the Izaak Walton League of America. But many other organizations, locally and nationally, hold stream-sampling workshops. These programs are great fun and are often geared for families with upper elementary, middle school, and high school kids. The Project Wild program (www.projectwild.org), sponsored by the national Council for Environmental Education, has a curriculum called Project Wild Aquatic, which teaches educators aquatic activities.

36 : BEES AND OTHER AWE-INSPIRING INSECTS

As I write this, I'm looking over sprays of wild aster—a gangly-looking wildflower that most neighbors probably assume is a weed. But if you look closely, you'll see that the plants are all beauty and buzz. The tiny flowers are swarming with bee flies, green bees, bumblebees, and myriad other insects. Looking beyond butterflies to see other insects is one of the easiest ways to slow down, sink in, and enjoy nature. You'll find insects with camouflage worthy of a National Geographic photo spread.

Flower Watching

Gather your kids and find each one a cluster of flowers to observe. Look for patches of flowers buzzing with insects. Pale white and purple flowers, such as those on mint species, are often a draw for native bees and related insects. In fall, goldenrod is crawling with stunning creatures, including the locust borer beetle. But any flower patch or flower bush frequented by insects will do.

Have each family member settle at a flower patch, or settle all together at one patch. Approach slowly and quietly, and sit as close as is comfortable without disturbing the flight patterns and behavior of the insects. As long as observers are quiet and not erratic in their movements, the bees, wasps, and other nectar-drinking insects should pay attention to the flower, not the person. Children should observe quietly for ten minutes and write or draw what they see and hear.

Here are some of the general kinds of creatures one might see visiting flowers.

Bumblebees

There are hundreds of bumblebee species. You can tell them apart by their sizes, colors, and numbers of stripes. Noticing and wondering about these stripes is what first led me to research about bumblebees and ultimately to write a children's book, *The Bumblebee Queen*.

Other Native Bees

Purplish, red, tiny, big, green, metallic—native bees are varied and stunning. Take a look. Stingless sweat bees may hover near you. Carpenter bees, which look like bumblebees, take up residence in wood. In our yard, it's not honeybees but bumblebees and tiny green bees that are the main insects pollinating blueberries. Having a nearby stand of native plants that supports these native pollinators can help in vegetable and fruit pollination. To find out more, consult the superb *Xerces Society Guide to Attracting Native Pollinators: Protecting North America's Bees and Butterflies*.

Bee Flies

If you see something that has the coloring of a bee or wasp but whose motion catches your eye, it may be a fly! Bee flies look remarkably like bees. But their habit of hovering and quickly moving from place to place will remind you of a housefly. And they have the many-faceted eyes of house flies. They don't sting. Looking for bee flies is a joy for kids who are fans of nifty camouflage.

Wasps

Getting to know wasps is one of the pleasures of insect watching. Unlike the quite aggressive German yellow jackets, most wasps we've encountered are quiet. Thread-waisted wasps and all manner of gorgeous orange and black wasps also hover near our flowers.

Hawk Moths

These hovering wonders look like hummingbirds. They're slightly fuzzy, like bumble-bees, but have oblong bodies.

Mosquitoes

Yes, mosquitoes frequent flowers. When female mosquitoes drink blood, they are preparing to reproduce. For daily nutrition, though, mosquitoes drink at flowers. I've never noticed any issues with being bitten by mosquitoes near flowers. The few I've seen seem quite intent on drinking nectar in the flower patch.

Have your kids take notes on, photograph, or draw insects they see. When looking at an insect, it often seems clear that you'll be able to remember its markings. But I can tell you from experience that five minutes later you'll likely forget whether it was striped red-then-black or black-then-red, and so on. The photos and notes you take will help, and are good to stretch your kids' vocabulary and overall language skills as they describe these creatures.

Living with Bees

When my nieces were young, they attended a Waldkindergärten ("forest kindergarten") school in Germany. It was all day, outdoors. One of the first things they learned was what they shouldn't bring for lunch. No sweetened drinks. No juices. No fruit. No gooey, sugary things. These attract wasps, yellow jackets, and bees. Yet what do most Americans do on a picnic? Break out the sodas. It's just asking for trouble. Drowning in a soda can, stepped on, or smashed by an unknowing child, a bee or wasp is likely to sting.

In late summer and early autumn, many wasps search for caterpillars and other small insects to take to their nests. During this time, the wasps seem a bit more aggressive and home in on meat products as well as fruits and juices. If you avoid these items in your picnic menu, you'll have a more pleasant outing for everyone.

Another method to help stay "bee safe" whenever you are in a wild outdoor habitat is to keep an eye out for bees and wasps coming and going in noticeable numbers. If they are entering and leaving a hole in the ground or other nest, don't step or garden near there. In our area, an introduced species called the German yellow jacket is aggressive in defending the nests it builds underground. It is easily bothered and will sting. (In southern states, Africanized honeybees are a species with which to be on guard.) Every other wasp species in our area is quite mellow. We've had small nests of paper wasps and mud dauber wasps right next to our doors in summer. They hover around but never become aggressive as we come and go, closing the door inches from their nest. My husband, Jeff, actually slapped his neck, found something there, pulled it off with his cupped hand, and opened his hand to find inside a bumblebee. It didn't sting. It just flew off. Wherever you live, the more you know about bees, wasps, and other insects, the more freely and comfortably you'll be able to walk in nature. You'll identify insects without getting flustered, and you'll more easily judge what is a sting danger and what is not.

37 : TOADALLY COOL

Toads are the ugly-beautiful stars of children's books. Their quiet nature (except during breeding season) makes them easy for kids to observe. My editor asked me who would want toads in a garden. Of course, my first thought was: who wouldn't want toads? Fact is, kids love toads and slugs and snails with a passion that is hard to explain. Lots of kids, if not taught to dislike these creatures, are immediately fascinated by them. (Maybe it's because kids have to sit around and wait a lot. Toads do, too!) And no, toads do not cause warts.

Toads need water and toads need mud. Toads need shade and time. Bring on toads if you don't mind fewer slugs. Slugs eat garden plants, so your gardening goals and those of toads might align. (Of course, a few slugs around are fun—kids have a definite fascination for them. Go out at night with a flashlight and see if you have some shiny slug trails in your grass and garden!)

Search for toads in cool, wet spots—under steps, shrubs, in mud. A downturned clay flowerpot can be a spot for a toad. Logs left to rot in a quiet corner can invite a toad for shade. Moss and fungi (mushrooms) are indicators of likely wet spots where toads might take up residence. (Or just follow the slugs—one of their food sources—to find toads.)

Consider cultivating a few moist habitats in your yard for the benefit of toads. Leave an area to overgrow, or a bit of mud, or a trench, or a scoop of soil where water runs off a downspout. In cold regions, toads need soil to dig into to spend the winter. (In desert areas, they need sandy soils to dig into during the hot, dry season.)

The trick with toads is to watch your step. Because, sometimes, they really won't get out of the way. Having a "toad abode" or "toad corner," a special place where kids walk slowly, carefully, respectfully, and watch for toads can add a new dimension to the garden and your family's routine. Creating loud and quiet areas, fast and slow areas, in a garden is not just about what plants we plant or paths we create but how we decide to act, as well.

Toads need to reproduce, and for that a nearby water source is beneficial. A wildlife pool or access to a pond is helpful. Toads may travel quite a distance to reproduce and then return to your yard.

If you're going to spray pesticides, don't bother to invite toads to your yard. They absorb chemicals very easily through their skin, so they're particularly vulnerable to non-natural chemicals such as pesticides. Plus, you're poisoning their food source— insects and slugs. (One more thing about toad and frog skin. Kids should have hands free of mosquito repellant, sunblock, and any other pore-clogging chemicals if they handle toads. Also, know toad and frog species before handling them. A few frog and toad species, mostly in tropical areas, exude poisons from their skin. Like most wild creatures, frogs and toads are best watched, not handled.)

Two books that are great to pair with toad and slug studies are *Wolfsnail* by Sarah Campbell and *The Snail's Spell* by Joanne Ryder.

Desert Puddles for Desert Toads

Desert-dwelling nature gardeners can join in the toad fun: surprisingly, toads live in US and Mexican deserts—and Australian deserts, too. The time to look for toads is after rain. Chances are, in the deserts of southwestern North America, you'll hear the Couch's spadefoot toads calling. They live most of the year underground then dig out when there is a substantial, puddle-making rain. They lay eggs in the rain puddles. Sonoran green toads, Sonoran desert toads, western narrowmouth toads, and red-spotted toads also live and reproduce in the desert Southwest. Urban Tucson, Arizona, is particularly rich in toads; it has frogs and toads of six different species.

If you live in the desert environment, you can help toads by creating a puddle-ready area. Just make a small depression in the soil and line it with water-garden rubber. If the rubber is dark, cover the bottom and sides with light-colored gravel so the pond will not heat up as much.

Let the natural rain fill it up and you might just get toads. Your lined area will last longer than a natural desert puddle. (Many natural puddles dry out in the hot sun, leaving tadpoles stranded without water.) So your puddle may help more toads hatch and develop before the desert sun dries it.

Amazingly, spadefoot toads have to call, find mates, lay eggs, and eat enough in just a few short weeks to last them the rest of the year, when they are in estivation, underground. Estivation is like hibernation, except it occurs during dry seasons, not cold ones. In both cases, the animals' breathing, heart rate, and overall metabolism slow so that very little energy is used. For a children's story about the spadefoot toad, see my book *Dig, Wait, Listen: A Desert Toad's Tale.*

38 : BATS ARE BEAUTIFUL

Bats' staccato flaps and zigzag flight make them cheer-worthy. Most kids would agree: bats are cool! Watching bats in the evening sky is a fun family activity. Bats are great insect catchers, and a substantial amount of what they capture is mosquitoes. Some bats, primarily tropical ones, feed on nectar or fruit.

Bats in the United States roost—hang out—in caves, hollow trees, crevices of bridge overhangs. Some species nest in colonies; others hang out individually. In some areas, bats show up in attics and chimneys because of the scarcity of natural nesting spots. Special bat-nesting boxes can be attached to houses, trees, and even bridges. What you can do to help bats depends on which kind live in your area.

Helping Bats

For information on bats and building or purchasing a bat house, one excellent resource is Bat Conservation International (www.batcon.org). BCI partners with vendors who sell a wide range of bat-friendly products, from bat houses that will hold about a dozen bats to a "bat mansion" that could hold 150. The inside of a bat house has rough surfaces where bat claws can cling. The houses are installed twelve to fifteen feet above the ground, with a wide open area for bats entering and leaving. Bat houses are most successful near water.

You can also garden for bats. Plant night-blooming flowers that provide nectar bats drink or attract insects bats eat. Bat-attracting plants include salvia, silene, phlox, cornflower, spearmint, moonflower, nicotiana, and four o'clocks. A local nature center or botanical garden may have recommendations for what suits your area. Many desert cacti attract bats. Of course, if you live in Arizona, you may find that your hummingbird feeders are mysteriously emptying at night. It could be bats taking a slurp!

Part Four

BRINGING IN THE BIRDS

You can plant a garden of colorful flowers. But how about a garden of colors that fly? To create that garden, just garden with birds in mind. The berry eaters. The seed eaters. The nectar drinkers. The insect snatchers. Let them swoop and swerve and flutter, providing yellows, reds, greens, and blues to fill your wild garden sky.

39 : BERRY EATERS

Who are the berry eaters? You may know them by purple stains on their breast feathers and beaks. Cedar waxwings are champion berry eaters. Yet lots of birds take advantage of berries when they are available. Robins that usually feed on worms will gather in pokeberry bushes in fall. Warblers, which have tiny bills and hunt mostly caterpillars and spiders in spring, eat lots of berries during fall migration. Bluebirds, famed for swooping in to eat insects from lawns, eat berries, too. Chipmunks, blue jays, wrens, foxes, raccoons—all manner of wild animals—will gobble berries you provide.

Berry Good Foods—for Wildlife

Some berries that can be eaten by wildlife are poisonous to people. Pokeberries are a good example. Pokeberry plants pop up, unasked for, and grow four feet tall or so. Lots of folks consider them weeds. But have you ever really looked at one? Their stems are dramatic pink; their berries a deep blue. If they weren't so common, people would likely plant them as treasured specimens. Migratory bird flocks feed on these important berries for nourishment. We leave big patches of them in less-manicured areas; just be sure to let the plants stay throughout the late fall and early winter so the birds can feast on them.

Myrtle warblers (also called yellow-rumped warblers) winter quite far north, in coastal Virginia, because they can dine on tiny myrtle berries and bayberries in winter. Most warblers can't. Myrtle warblers' bodies are specially adapted to digest the waxy berries of wax myrtle and bayberries. (How waxy are the berries? Traditional bayberry candles are actually made from these fragrant berries' wax!)

Other popular wildlife food berries of the eastern half of the United States are wild blackberries and serviceberries. Serviceberry trees are excellent ornamentals. Wild grapes, Virginia creeper, even poison ivy berries are bird food. Berries and berry-like wild fruits of the desert and dry southwestern regions include desert hackberry, gray thorn, wolfberry, sumac, madrone, juniper, and chokecherry. To find out about good wildlife berries in your area, contact your local fish and wildlife department or native plant nursery.

It's best to plant native berry-producing plants. Native or non-native, berry plants spread. Birds eat the berries. Some of the tiny seeds in berries survive the trip through the birds' digestive systems. They're deposited, here and there, with a dollop of fertilizer, provided by the birds' droppings.

The Importance of the Last Morsel

Wildlife gardeners plant mostly what creatures love: the holly berries that waxwings devour or the elderberry bushes that will attract a flock of migrating birds. Yet an ecologist acquaintance taught me a lesson. We were walking his eighty-acre property, looking at the forest, prairie, and wetland. I asked about his wildlife plants. He pointed out a highbush cranberry. I said, "Our birds don't like them much. Barely touch a one." Perhaps my tone of voice showed my attitude.

That's when he explained. "You know, it's important to have some plants like that—the berries the birds don't just eat right away. That's because they are left, unpicked in fall. During a hard winter, those berries will still be on the bush, and after a few freezes and thaws they'll soften up and be ready for eating." We've found this to be true with other fruits, too. Ornamental crabapple trees go untouched most years. But sometimes, on an icy day in February or March, hungry robins will show up and devour every last tiny crabapple. The freezing and thawing during winter softens the crabapples. Hawthorn and holly are helpful for late winter feeding, as well.

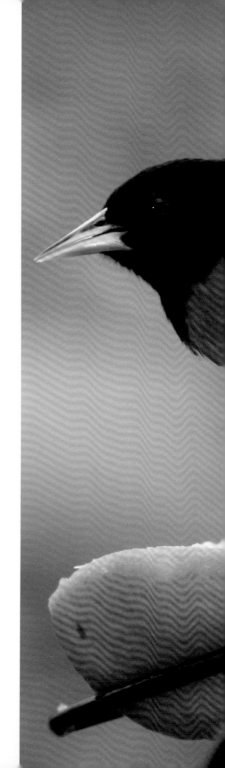

40 : SHARING BERRIES
WITH THE BIRDS

One college summer, I worked at a nature day camp in Ivoryton, Connecticut. A few of us were walking down a trail and came upon wild raspberries. I began picking them—perhaps with a bit too much relish.

"Leave some for the birds," said the chief naturalist. The idea surprised me. I hadn't thought of the birds, probably hiding in the trees and bushes. Perhaps they were waiting, counting on this food to survive. For me, the berries were just a treat, a welcome addition to whatever was in the dining hall. But to the birds—those berries might be life. I blushed. I'd thought I was such an environmentalist, so aware of nature. But I was only just beginning to walk with respect and see the world with wild creatures' needs in mind.

Edible Landscaping for You and Wildlife

We all love berries. So why not combine some of your wildlife gardening with yummy family fun? If you're planting bushes, why not blueberry bushes? If you're putting down ground cover, why not cranberries? If you need a small decorative tree, why not plant a cherry or apple? Edible landscaping is fun and has a tasty payoff. Just be prepared for your possessive side to be challenged.

My mom, a fierce gardener, knew she shared the sour cherry tree with the birds. She'd grumble, wave her arms to scare off the robins as we approached the cherry tree, and perhaps give them a talking to. But then she'd relent, "I'm leaving the high ones for you," she'd say as we picked what we could and the robin families did, too. If all goes well, you'll be donating quite a number of the edible berries you plant to wildlife.

The thing is, the pleasure of edible wild landscaping is not the amount of fruit these plants bear. It's this feeling of bonus. Of power. When you step out your door and eat a few berries off your bush, tree, or ground cover, you feel as if you've been given a sweet, free bite. Your kids can have that Easter-egg-hunt anticipation, watching for fruit that ripens. It's just such a connected feeling to eat a bit of home-grown food.

As I write this, I'm looking out on our blackberry plant. Two cardinals and a catbird have been sampling bites. A juvenile scarlet tanager just checked out a cherry tomato. Would I rather eat that cherry tomato or see a scarlet tanager? See a scarlet tanager, of course! I can be generous. And that catbird, in its graceful graphite plumage, is poking at *my* blackberries. "Hey—!" Oh well. I happily watch it preen. Thankfully, I have the South Bend Farmer's Market to back me up with produce. I'll take a photo of that catbird for the book. That's a fair exchange, isn't it? As always, in wildlife gardening, we strike our own balance between our needs and those of other creatures.

Fruit for You and Wildlife

To find fruit for your yard, check the usual gardening sources: catalogs and nurseries. You probably have a nursery that specializes in fruit for your area. If you're interested in blackberries or raspberries, cultivate some gardening friends. They're likely to have plenty of "starts" (young plants) for you. (Contact local gardening clubs; many older and experienced gardeners could use a bit of help from the strong hands and sharp eyes of young gardeners-in-training. Many will share their knowledge and the plants that volunteer, ready-to-dig, in a mature garden.)

Here are a few general guidelines for finding plants that work well for both gardeners and wildlife.

Raspberries

Raspberries are incredibly easy to grow and don't need perfect full sun. Fair warning: they spread quickly. So you have to have the space and willingness to do continuing maintenance, or else have a low-key attitude about plants that do their own thing. In our experience, red raspberries aren't a big favorite among the birds. A few will peck at them; the plants also attract daddy longlegs and a variety of beautiful moths. So most red raspberries will be for humans—not a bad thing. Black raspberries, in contrast, are a preferred bird food in our area. (The black raspberries occur wild here; there are domesticated varieties, too.) We pick a few but leave many for the catbirds, who sing us their beautiful songs. But which berries will be eaten and which will be left by wildlife is a very localized phenomenon. It depends on the animals in your area and the local food supplies available to them.

Blackberries

Blackberries spread more slowly than raspberries, but they're still vigorous and easy to grow. They make new plants when their canes (the long stems) touch the ground and take root. They're easier to control than raspberries if you keep an eye on the canes. Keep those

tied up above the ground, or cut ones that are rooting if you don't want to begin a new plant. Still, blackberries can get ahead of you. For that reason, I'd recommend planting thornless varieties instead of thorny ones. They taste just as delicious.

Birds love blackberries. Inspect the berries you eat. There may be a bird bite out of the back of many. Too bad the birds don't just bite one berry but taste many, instead! Cardinals, catbirds, and even tanagers flock to our berries. The plants produce so thickly, though, that there are some berries left for us, as well.

Blueberries

Highbush blueberries are quite specific about the soil conditions they need. But if you have acid soil, or are willing to add organic fertilizers to create the right conditions, they can grow for you. They become big bushes over time. The bushes will attract birds and children. Share the berries if you can. Just plant plenty, because the robins may gather. Waxwings may stop by. Enjoy eating and bird watching at these plants.

Cranberries

Cranberries provide the kind of low-growing, lovely ground cover that would be perfect for a garden bed. However, they grow incredibly slowly and need specific soil conditions, as blueberries do. They are native to bogs. It would be an expensive proposition to cover much area with cranberry unless you really lived in the perfect habitat. (I've tried. I ended up putting in creeping thyme, which spreads more quickly, feels soft underfoot, and provides late July flowers for bees and butterflies.)

Currants

If you have a sunny spot, currants are easy to grow. They'll attract wildlife, as well. Chipmunks may climb up to munch berries. Birds will stop by. Just a few bushes can provide abundant berries for wildlife and your family. Toss these tart berries on salads, or just enjoy watching the birds feast outdoors.

Apple and Pear

Apple and pear trees provide early blossoms for bumblebees. The organic trees in our yard also seem to provide plenty of caterpillars for birds later on. But they're not a haven for wildlife the way cherry trees are.

Nut Trees

Pecan, walnut, beech, and other nut trees attract squirrels, deer, javelinas (peccaries), bears, and other creatures. Nuts are a rich wildlife food. Plan thoughtfully if you plant nut trees, because some of these varieties grow very large. Black walnut trees release chemicals from their roots that discourage other plants from growing nearby—so don't plan to have your garden under the walnut's branches. Also, walnuts have a thick outer husk over the shell that we usually see on walnuts in the grocery store. A natural walnut is quite a heavy projectile and, of course, these fall to the ground from a great height. Don't plant a walnut tree right over your children's play area—or they'll have to stay out from under it during the fall season.

Cherries

Cherry trees are always a hit with wildlife. Waxwings, robins, tanagers, robins, and red-bellied woodpeckers will flock to dine at a tart cherry tree in fruit. You can buy dwarf varieties, so you can easily reach the branches to pick all the cherries. Well—not all. Know upfront that the birds may get the biggest share. With wildlife gardening, that's half the fun! Wild cherry trees produce a lot of fruit as well, but the berries are very small and really enjoyable only to wildlife.

Cherry trees, both wild and domestic, are host to a variety of caterpillars that become beautiful butterflies. In the eastern and midwestern United States, the tiger swallowtail, a huge yellow-and-black butterfly, grows up on cherry leaves. Some butterflies lay eggs on the tender-leaved, small cherry saplings, so keep some of these around, or continue cutting back a small wild cherry tree so that it has new growth each year. The young, small leaves on cherry saplings, close to the ground, will give your kids a place to hunt for caterpillars. Tent caterpillars and fall webworms often take up residence in cherry trees. But healthy trees can usually handle the population of caterpillars, and after they finish feeding, the tree will recover without any action on the part of the homeowner.

41 : WELCOME, SEEDEATERS

Seeds are nutrient-rich foods that help animals survive. Cardinals, nutcrackers, blue jays, grosbeaks, goldfinches, and many other birds are primarily seedeaters. (Their short, stout, seed-cracking bills are a clue to what they eat.) That's why people put out seed feeders for these birds. But there are natural "seed feeders"—plants. And you don't have to buy seed or clean and fill these feeders. So why not choose plants, not just for flowers but for their seeds?

Sunflowers of all sorts are prime wildlife food. So are thistle seeds. That's why bird feeders filled with these seeds are so effective. Other seed-providing plants favored by wildlife have surprised us. The seeds are so small that we wouldn't expect them to be food. Yet when the tall purple spikes of liatris form seed, goldfinches move to these plants.

It's fun to watch the plant stems sway as finches settle to dine. This year, in mid-October, a migratory flock of white-throated sparrows feasted on the miniscule seeds of native asters. Finding out what plants provide seed in your garden is a matter of trial and error. Consulting an experienced gardener or bird watcher in your area may give you some clues to the best plants. Coneflowers such as purple coneflower, the source of echinacea, have seeds that birds eat. In the desert habitat, desert false indigo and big saltbush are important wildlife food.

Often gardeners "deadhead" flowers, meaning they pluck the wilted flowers from the plant, so it will put its energy into making more flowers, not seed. This does work, creating more flowers and food for butterflies. But, to encourage seed production, stop deadheading. Let the flowers pass, allow plants to make seed, and then discover new colors in the garden: the flying, songbird kind!

The Sunflower Race

Sunflower seeds are relatively big and easy for young fingers, just getting coordinated, to handle. They're a perfect first plant for young children to grow. Sunflower plants are natural wildlife feeders. Some varieties will grow to tower over the kids, so they're definitely an impressive early project. Buy several seed varieties, of several heights, and see which grow best and which suit the birds best. If you have any native species of sunflowers in your area, buy seeds and plants of those as well.

Once you and your children have planted the seeds,

according to the directions on the seed packets, the sunflower race starts. Which plants grow fastest, tallest? As the race is on, have your kids keep weekly charts to follow the progress of the plants. When the flowers have fully formed, that race is over.

Another race begins. Which sunflower seed head will be cleaned out first by wildlife? Birds will begin to pick. Chipmunks and mice may climb up and help. (If a raccoon or squirrel carries off an entire seed head . . . well, perhaps that's a win.)

If your young gardeners are eager, set up a time-lapse sequence of photos. Have each of the kids stand beside a few sunflowers for a photo. For the first day, have them hold up a sign indicating what week it is in the sunflower's growth. (Try to remember to have a week-one photo, with nothing showing from the ground.) Take another photo, same child and same plant, with a "two weeks" sign a week later. Continue all summer long. Then string together the photos for a slideshow or PowerPoint presentation and you'll have a fun time-lapse view of sunflowers popping up and towering over the kids. Just make sure you show several sunflowers in the picture, in case some don't sprout and grow as you had hoped.

Rethinking Bird Feeders

As much fun as bird feeders are, a broad array of wildlife plantings that provide seeds and berries is probably a bit more healthy for birds. On a berry bush or seed plant, the animals are rarely as closely packed as on a seed feeder, so their chances of attracting a predator are reduced. Also, bird feeders need cleaning, and the birds are in such close proximity that the spread of diseases among birds is more likely than when they're hopping in a bush or tree.

If you're hoping to purely benefit wildlife, and not going to be around for much wildlife viewing close to the feeder, wildlife plantings, not putting up feeders, is the way to go. If you're able to view the feeders a lot and will have pleasure from watching birds at feeders, then bird feeding is likely worth the extra work and care. Consult the local Audubon Society or wild bird feeding store for feeders suited to the birds of your habitat.

42 : SYMPHONY OF SEEDS

Seeds are plants in action. Seeds perform. They float and fly. They hitch rides on animals. They offer entertainment to your kids after the flowers have gone. Below are some plants that benefit wildlife but also have seeds that are particularly enjoyable for kids.

Jewelweed

One good patch of jewelweed not only feeds the hummingbirds; it also gives kids daily pleasure in late summer and fall, as they gently activate the seed pods. With the slight brush of your finger, the jewelweed pods throw seeds far and wide.

Lupine

Lupine—native plants that produce lavender spikes of flowers—have intriguing seeds, too. As they dry, they suddenly twist and spring open, throwing seeds into the air and onto the surrounding soil. Look for volunteer plants to pop up nearby the next year.

Milkweed

Milkweeds are a childhood favorite when it comes to seed entertainment. These plants, so important to butterflies and beetles, produce small, light seeds attached to feathery white down. As the pods open, take a look at the elegant way the seeds are packed inside. Then pull out the fluff and have a family dance, flinging the milkweed seeds and letting them float in the air until they've found a place to rest and, perhaps, sprout. Does the floating fluff remind you of anything?

In the 1940s Disney movie *Fantasia*, during the "Waltz of the Flowers" from the *Nutcracker* suite, Autumn Fairies touch milkweed pods, which turn into what look like ballerinas dancing. The fluff is the white skirts, and the dancers' bodies are the dark seeds.

Milkweed down has also been used for pillow stuffing. Goldfinches use the down to line their nests in late summer. There are many milkweed species, adapted for various habitats. Some good books to follow up your seed fun would be *Monarch and Milkweed* by Helen Frost, *Flip, Float, Fly: Seeds on the Move* by JoAnn Early Macken, and *A Seed Is Sleepy* by Dianna Hutts Aston.

Cottonwood

A seed star of many riparian (riverside) habitats is the cottonwood. Cottonwood trees grow tall along rivers through many otherwise treeless areas in the western United States. In the Midwest, we have cottonwood, too. (There are several species and these vary, place to place.) Cottonwood seeds, which have fluffy down like a short milkweed, begin to fall in the first week of June—seemingly from far off in the sky. That's because the trees are so tall the down can fly quite a long distance. Once it reaches the ground, ants busily gather the seeds. The trees are songbird habitat in the western United States. They're also important shelter for creatures such as moose and deer.

Conifers

Of course, it's not just seeds themselves that provide entertainment. Pinecones and other cones that hold seeds are great for crafts and all-around fun. Conifers have wildlife value, too. From the longleaf pines of the southeastern United States to the whitebark pine, ponderosa pine, limber pine, and Douglas firs of the western mountains, conifers produce both shelter for wildlife and seeds for wildlife to eat. Birds such as Clark's nutcrackers and crossbills pry apart the cones to get at the seeds inside. Finding conifers for your habitat involves some garden experimentation, reading up on local wildlife, and talking with local wildlife experts and enthusiasts.

43 : INSECT EATERS

One day my husband and I looked out and saw a woodchuck eating our milkweed plants, right during monarch-caterpillar season. Jeff ran out to chase it off. He returned and said, "I know it's weird to get upset at an animal for eating a plant just so we can save it for another animal that's going to eat the plant." His comment reflects some of the goofy choices wildlife gardeners find themselves making as they balance wildlife needs, and our human preferences, in a habitat.

So, wildlife lovers, prepare to puzzle your friends a bit more. Choose a plant that's likely to get infested with insects. Why insects? Why, to attract insect eaters, of course! New Jersey tea, a native prairie shrub, attracts a haze of tiny insects to its small white flowers. It's a magnet for both flycatchers and hummingbirds. (Hummingbirds eat not just nectar but also insects. Hunting dragonflies may stop by, too.) That oozing, insect-full plant you think is "sick" may actually be a wildlife feeding ground.

Oak trees are stately and provide acorns and shade. Yet, to warblers, their great value is in what infests them: oak-loving insects. In the midwestern United States, just as warblers are passing through, in late April and early May, oak trees begin to leaf out. Oak-eating insects begin to squirm. These caterpillars are food for warblers. The ornithologists Jean and Richard Graber estimated that warblers can eat as much as 1.7 times their weight in caterpillars each day. The birds need these trees as food sources for caterpillars. Cherry trees, too, host many caterpillars and provide a feeding ground for later caterpillar eaters.

To feed bluebirds, many homeowners provide insect-hunting habitats: pesticide-free lawns, grasslands, bushes, and trees. Since berries make up about 30 percent of bluebirds' diet, bird lovers should also provide plants with fruit such as serviceberry, elderberry, blackberry, viburnum, and crabapple. But some folks sure love their bluebirds. They take it a bit further, by directly feeding insects to the birds. They put a small saucer of living mealworms on a regular platform feeder, porch railing, or other spot. The birds swoop in and eat the insects. This supplies the birds with extra food when food is scarce; mostly, though, it gives people the pleasure of seeing the birds up close as the bluebirds come in to feed. Check with stores that supply bird feeders, bird seed, and other products; most sell mealworms, as well. Mealworms can also be ordered on the Internet.

44 : HELLO, HUMMINGBIRDS!

If you visit the indoor hummingbird exhibit at the Arizona—Sonora Desert Museum, you may become part of the exhibit. During nesting season, hummingbirds sometimes pull hair from people's heads or threads from their clothes to use in building nests.

But when the exhibit first opened, the birds had a hard time building nests. The exhibit was in a new building. The curators provided the birds with native plants, plenty of mosses, bark, and lichen for their nest-building. Still, the nests the birds built weren't holding together. They were falling apart and not well fastened to the branches.

Finally, a curator figured out what was wrong. The building was so new it had no spiders in it. Without spider webs, the hummingbirds couldn't build proper, secure nests. Spider webs are a perfect sticky wrapping; they hold the nests together. The spider web fibers also stretch—so as the chicks grow, the nest accommodates the chicks' growing size! To fix the problem, the curator had to gather spider webs and spiders from outdoors and bring them into the new exhibit space. How hummingbirds build their nests is just one of the many curiosities of these birds. In behavior and biology, they are full of surprises.

Feeders and Plants

To lure hummingbirds to your yard, you could put out a hummingbird feeder. But putting one up is a commitment. You have to keep the feeder clean, otherwise you'll harm the birds more than help them. (See the feeder care instructions at the end of this chapter.) In the long term, installing plants for hummingbirds is actually a lower maintenance project than using feeders. Even if you put up a hummingbird feeder, you'll probably want to plant hummingbird flowers to increase your chances of attracting hummingbirds.

The best hummingbird plants vary from region to region. Plants such as trumpet vine may seem like a great choice. But these vines take over an area, and if you plant one you may spend decades, without success, trying to hack back their roots and contain them. For that reason, you should only plant them if you have a big area and don't mind it a bit wild. What works in one area may be a pest plant in another. Don't be reluctant to ask local experts for help.

In a desert garden in Arizona, you might plant western red columbine, bearded penstemon, desert honeysuckle, ocotillo, agave, and Texas sage. In our garden in the Midwest, native red honeysuckle and red columbine are good choices. In the Midwest and Northeast, columbine, cardinal flower, red honeysuckle, coral bells, and bee balm work well. In the Southeast, bee balm, pineapple sage, and firebush are among the best hummingbird plants. Ask for advice about plants from a nature center or native plant society. But you and your kids can also seek out hummingbird plants on your own. You just have to look for clues.

Hummingbirds eat more than just nectar. They eat insects—so any plant that attracts small, gnat-like insects may appeal to hummingbirds. And, as mentioned in the food sources chapter (chapter 8, "What's on the Menu?"), hummingbirds drink tree sap. With their small bills they can't drill holes for sap, but they will lick sap from already existing tree cracks or holes drilled by sapsuckers—a kind of woodpecker. If you'd like to attract these beautiful birds to your area, plant trees that produce plenty of sap. Birches, hemlocks, maples, and willows are favored sapsucker trees. If sapsuckers "like" (and lick) a tree to the point where the tree's health is suffering, you may have to cover some of its trunk with hardware cloth or other tree wrapping to reduce their activity.

Features of Hummingbird Flowers

Hummingbirds are attracted to flowers that provide a lot of slightly sweet nectar. Hummingbird flowers are trumpet-shaped or vase-shaped. Hummingbird flowers often hang down because hummingbirds can hover to feed. Hummingbird flowers tend to be red, but many are white or yellow. Purple flowers, such as those on sage or mint, are more attractive to bees. Many hummingbird flowers have no smell at all.

A trumpet-shaped flower that blooms at night is probably not a hummingbird flower. It's likely a bat or moth flower, instead. A common example sold widely is datura. Bat-pollinated flowers tend to be large and have a strong smell, sometimes like rotting fruit. (By the way, bats help pollinate mangos and guavas. Thank you, bats!)

Of course, hummingbirds don't read rule books about what flowers to visit. Every time naturalists state a rule, it seems that wild creatures go out and break it. Truth is, some species can eat a variety of foods and adapt to what is available.

For example, butterflies, hummingbirds, and moths visit butterfly bush, or buddleia, which lives in our yard. This great plant, originally from China, dies off in cold winters in our area, so it doesn't spread far and is a manageable garden plant. Unfortunately, it does too well in some habitats. In Washington state, for instance, it's invaded many wild areas and outcompeted local plant species.

Flower Detectives

Try a hummingbird "field trip" to a local park, botanical garden, or garden center. Have your wildlife helpers take turns looking for hummingbird flowers, bee flowers, or butterfly flowers. Have them compete—for fun. If you need to make it more rigorous, have them take photos of each kind of flower and make a chart, on the computer, or on paper plates or posters, of what kinds of flowers suit each kind of creature.

If you're visiting the Desert Botanical Garden in Phoenix, Arizona, you can kick off your studies by looking at the Bee Garden, Hummingbird Garden, and Butterfly Garden there, then spread out to examine flowers in other gardens on the site. Some other botanical gardens and zoos in North America have wildlife garden exhibits, as well.

Hummingbird Feeder Care

If you do put up a hummingbird feeder, keep the following pointers in mind:

Do not use red food coloring in the nectar (or any coloring at all). It's not necessary, and some anecdotal evidence suggests that it's not good for the birds. To play it safe, avoid it. Natural flower nectar does not contain red dye, so why give it to the birds? Hummingbird feeders have red parts that will attract the birds. The entire bottle does not need to be red.

To make hummingbird nectar, mix four parts water to one part sugar. (For example, that would be 1 cup of water to ¼ cup granulated white sugar.) Boil briefly and cool.

Pour it into the feeder. Wipe the outside of the feeder thoroughly, so it's not sticky and attractive to bees. Never use sugar substitutes, as the sweet taste will still be attractive to the birds but provide zero nutrition. Hummingbirds are not on a diet. They need the calories to survive.

Once every week to ten days, clean the feeder in your mud room or kitchen sink. A pipe cleaner or bottle scrubber will help clean out the small holes. The important thing is to get rid of the mold. A solution of ten parts water to one part bleach will sterilize it. A simple way to accomplish this is to use a bleach pen. Drip a bit of the bleach solution into a small quantity of water or on the feeder and rinse it, over and over. Wipe it dry to make doubly sure there's no bleach on the feeder.

A few insects in the nectar aren't a problem. But you don't want the feeder to be a death trap for native bees and other insects. We have a disc-shaped feeder and fill it only halfway to the feeding slits. This is far enough below the feeding holes so that bees' and wasps' tongues can't reach the nectar, but hummingbird tongues can. The result is that very few wasps come to the feeders. We learned this trick from the people who feed hummingbirds at the Nature Conservancy's famed hummingbird hotspot, Ramsey Canyon in Arizona.

If you live in an area that has bats, leave your feeder out for them to enjoy, too. But if you have bears around, take those feeders inside at night. You don't want to be a bear feeder by accident!

45 : A BUILDING MATERIALS BUFFET FOR THE BIRDS

One day my grandmother went to fetch laundry from the line and found twigs sticking out of the pocket of Grandfather's jean overalls. A wren was eyeing her from a bush. Soon, she saw the bird back in the pocket, at work on its nest. Well, Grandmother appreciated home building of any sort. And that wren already had the pocket half filled. What could she do but leave Grandfather's overalls on the line for several weeks?

The female wren laid eggs, and the wren family grew up in that pocket. Once they were fledged, there was some serious washing to do. I asked my mother what

Grandfather had said about his overalls being used in such a fashion. She said, "Well, I don't expect Grandmother asked him. I just hope he had some other pants to wear." Knowing Grandfather, I'm sure he got a kick out of that wren's choice of nesting site, too.

Starting the Buffet

Flowers and food sources aren't the only ways to attract birds to your yard. Offering shelter is another way to support the birds. When people think of helping birds nest, they usually think of building birdhouses out of wood. Yet there's a way you and your family can help them without a saw, hammer, or nails. Just provide materials they need to build their nests.

A good way to start is to research the local birds and what kind of building materials they need for nests. But if you have some eager wildlife helpers, skip that step. Experiment. Provide materials. See what the birds choose.

Decide where you're going to set out your "building materials buffet." It's fun to put them up on a picnic table, rock, or tree so you can easily see if there are any "takers." Or you can hang them in a tree. Make sure this area is visible from a window in your house. Having the building materials buffet up, away from predators, also makes it easier for birds to comfortably gather materials and fly away. Consider it an informal wildlife experiment. (Take notes, if you like. It could be set up as a science fair project, complete with charts, photos, and pictures.) Below are some tips on what materials you might provide.

Twig Race

For fun, have a timed race to gather small twigs, pencil-sized or much smaller in diameter. Who can find ten first? Gather these for your building materials buffet.

Furry Fun

Gather clumps of pet hair. (It's a good time to groom the dog.) These can be placed right out on a surface, or you can put them in a mesh bag, such as an old onion bag. Birds can pull out the fur through the holes. An old basket works, too.

Make It Mud!

Take a shallow pan, mix up some mud, and set it out for the birds. Will they use it? It depends on what species live in your area and how available mud is. In March 2011, Britain's Royal Society for the Protection of Birds recommended that British bird lovers put out mud, because Britain was experiencing a long period without rain. House swallows and martins build their homes out of mud, often cementing them to the eaves of houses and barns. Without the usual spring mud puddles, the birds were having trouble finding material to repair their old nests or make new ones. Humans stepped in to help.

Keep the Stems

This part of your building materials buffet takes some advance thinking, year to year. Notice which plants animals use for their nests. In spring, a bird busily tugging at a plant is a good sign it's gathering nesting materials. In our yard, orioles climb up and down swamp milkweed plants, pulling fibers from the stems to make their nests. Now that we know their preference, we leave these dead plant stems from the previous year standing in our formal flower gardens. Another common plant fiber is that of grapevine. Birds don't typically use the whole vine. Songbirds pull the outer fibers from the vine and use them in their nests.

Fluff Preferred

Some species line their nests with the wispy fluff that carries seeds such as milkweed and dogbane through the air. American goldfinches use the fluff from thistles—called thistledown—for that purpose. They are late nesters, as they must wait until the thistle has been pollinated and the seeds are fully developed before their preferred nesting material is available. If you have plants that provide seed fluff of some type, watch it closely and see if any birds in your area use it for nesting. You'll then know which plants should remain standing after they have gone to seed. (Although there are many excellent native types of thistle, highly invasive Canada thistle has choked many wetlands. This species should not be allowed to grow or set seed in your wildlife habitat.)

"No" to Dryer Lint

Wildlife experts used to suggest that people put out dryer lint for birds to use in their nests. Although birds will use this material, providing it is no longer recommended. For one thing, dryer lint may compact and harden when it's rained on. That just makes a mucky wet nest for the chicks. For another thing, dryer lint is covered with soaps and other chemical residues. And finally, most people have polyester fleece and other synthetic fabrics among their clothes. Putting tiny pieces of these difficult-to-biodegrade materials out in the environment, and in the young birds' nests, is less than ideal. (This is not to say that birds won't choose to put plastic pieces in their nests on their own.)

Leave the Lichen

Many of us know that standing dead trees, called snags, are important wildlife homes. They provide soft wood where animals can excavate nesting holes. But snags, fallen logs, and dead branches have another role, as raw materials. They are a growing surface for moss and lichen, which are used in nests. Don't harvest lichen and moss for the birds and put it in your buffet table; let them do it themselves. That way, the unused lichen and moss will stay where they live best and will continue to grow. Many lichens are extremely slow-growing.

46 : CAVITY NESTERS

Although some birds build their nests atop a tree's branches, many others nest in tree holes, called tree cavities. Some cavity nesters can excavate their own holes. Woodpeckers excavate holes flake by flake, over several weeks. After woodpeckers have abandoned the hole, chickadees, nuthatches, and bluebirds may use the hole for nesting. Large woodpeckers, such as hairy woodpeckers or pileated woodpeckers, may expand a tree hole excavated by a smaller woodpecker, or they may start their own. Later on, these woodpecker holes become nests for wood ducks, fox squirrels, flying squirrels, raccoons, and opossums.

Cavities are most easily drilled in softer wood. Weakened tree areas, such as where a branch has fallen, may become waterlogged and begin to rot away. Birds flake off bark and tug at wood splinters. Insects bore holes. Over time, all this activity weathers and

softens the area, which may naturally form a hole, with very little help from a woodpecker.

For these cavity nesters, trees, especially dead or partially dead trees, are the best kind of homes. But through experimentation, some wildlife watchers and conservationists have developed birdhouses that attract cavity nesters.

Wood duck houses are one of the biggest success stories. Chickadees take to birdhouses easily, too, as do owls, especially screech owls. Each kind of birdhouse must be made to the specific needs of the birds. The entrance hole usually has specific dimensions—in the case of songbirds, just large enough to let them in without allowing larger birds. Designs and directions for making nesting boxes are widely available in books, from conservation organizations such as Audubon, and on the web through various conservation sites. Stores specializing in bird feeders often stock, or can order, nesting boxes for various bird species.

Bluebirds are easily outcompeted for nesting cavities by non-native starlings, and even more often by European house sparrows. Even if the bluebirds have already taken up residence, European house sparrows may kick them out of the nest box, or attack and kill the adults or young. To encourage bluebirds to nest in an area, it's usually necessary to trap and remove European house sparrows from the nest boxes. Don't put up a bluebird house unless you're willing to take the responsibility of maintaining it.

Swallows, too, can take a bluebird's nesting spot. But swallows are native birds and need homes, as well. One

solution, surprisingly, is a dual swallow house—bluebird house. The two birdhouses are put back-to-back on the same fencepost. Swallows are likely to take up residence on one side, bluebirds on the other. (This technique does not always work, but it's worth a try; we've seen it used successfully all over our local state park.) Be sure to place bluebird houses three hundred feet apart; each pair needs that much territory. For information on setting up and maintaining a bluebird house, check with the North American Bluebird Society, www.nabluebirdsociety.org. You could also do an Internet search for "bluebird society" and your state name, to look for a local club with members who will help get you started with building and maintaining bluebird houses.

Another beloved insect eater, the purple martin, can be supported with nesting boxes or clusters of gourd houses. For information, check out the Purple Martin Conservation Association, http://purplemartin.org, which offers a wealth of detailed information on these birds' biology, where to site purple martin houses, and how to maintain them. The organization also has a catalog of related products and supplies some bluebird materials as well.

Part Five

A PLACE FOR PEOPLE: BEING PART OF YOUR WILDLIFE GARDEN

A wildlife garden is built to benefit wildlife. But part of the payoff is creating family memories, too. This section delves into the secrets of effective wildlife watching, offers tips on how to stay safe and comfortable in the garden, and suggests methods for deepening your family's relationship to nature.

47 : SECRETS TO SUCCESSFUL WILDLIFE WATCHING

It doesn't take an encounter with whales to make my day. Sometimes a bumblebee will do. In the warm sun, I watched one bee fly up inside a blueberry flower. Thanks to that bee, someday we'd have a blueberry. For that moment, my breath and the sun and the bee and the flower seemed all of a piece. It may have only been a few seconds, but the time in that space seemed long and strong.

Finding the stillness that allows this kind of deeper nature watching isn't always easy. Those golden moments are fleeting in a noisy, busy world. Yet learning wildlife watching skills can help your family sink deeper into the joy of being part of the wild.

There is a kind of dance to wildlife watching—a push and pull. You sense the animals, you learn their signals, you know their habits and routines. You learn to enter their environment and may even get to know an individual animal and how close it will allow you to come without it becoming disturbed.

To Freeze or Not

You might think that freezing in place is the best way to avoid disturbing animals. It is in some cases, but not always. In the suburban and urban environment, many creatures such as squirrels, chipmunks, skunks, and birds are accustomed to people as part of their habitat. People walk on sidewalks right past tree squirrels and woodchucks all the time. These animals don't become alarmed until someone stops or steps off of the sidewalk. It's a sign that they've been noticed. *Then* they become concerned. And animals take cues from other animals. So if a deer stops suddenly, freezing in place, squirrels and birds look around to see what is amiss. If a human stops dramatically, wild animals check to see what's up, too!

Smooth Move!

Move slowly, but don't stalk. Your shape is important. Imagine you are a chipmunk. How does a human look, standing up? (From a chipmunk's perspective, a human may be mostly feet and tall stick legs. One can only speculate.) How does a human look, crouched down? Many urban and suburban wild creatures are used to humans walking around near them. But once you lean down to look, and see them eye to eye, they scurry away or hide. Crouching down, which we often do to seem friendly to a child, can actually be more threatening to a wild animal. A crouching animal, in the wild, is an animal that pounces and stalks. (Unless it's being submissive, as with pack animals such as wolves, which crouch to seem lower than the dominant animal.) There's no one way to act around animals. Each species is different. You have to get out there and find out what works with each creature.

Many animals are mellower than people think. My husband walked up to a skunk to let it out of a live trap, and it didn't bother him at all. We've had close encounters with lots of skunks, and they don't waste their spray on just anyone or anything. We saw raccoons and even woodchucks walk up to skunks with no negative interaction. The raccoons even pushed up against the sides of the skunks, as if they liked their smell! Still, the skunks didn't spray.

Now, I'm not recommending you walk up to a skunk. No, not at all. I'm just saying that some wild creatures have undeserved reputations. The main reason that people think skunks will spray anyone, anywhere, is that it's people with dogs who usually find skunks. And dogs bumble right up and threaten the skunks, even trying to grab them. No wonder they get skunked so often. Deer, in contrast, are more dangerous than you might think. If they are startled, those hooves can do damage. Pet only the domestic animals you know.

Watching without Staring

Have you ever had a feeling that someone is staring at you? It seems wild animals notice staring, too. Mammals, in general, don't like to be stared at. (At least that's been my observation over years of being around wild animals.) Sometimes it helps, when you're watching an animal, to look to the side of an animal, instead of directly at it, or to pretend you're busy with something else, even when you're not. The birds and other creatures may return to their activities.

Dressing the Part

In nature, colors have meanings. Red and pink are sometimes warning colors. It's best to dress in quiet colors for wildlife watching—try to choose milder, leafy colors, such as green, khaki, or brown. (Unless you want to attract hummingbirds, in which case bright colors are a good idea, indeed!)

One Animal, One You

Do wild animals know you? After a while, chances are, yes, they do. Studies have shown that crows learn individual faces and react to specific human facial features. (A scientist studied this by having students use masks. Certain masks always elicited the same reaction.) The squirrels in our yard definitely know us. The chickadees and nuthatches fly right to feeders after we've filled them up. When a hawk is in the area, and birds are reluctant to come to feeders, the birds will hop in when we're around, as if we are some kind of protection.

The animals seem to know my husband, Jeff, the best. As for me, I have to wear the same kinds of clothes and behave in the regular "human in the yard" way or they become noticeably concerned. This is another advantage of having outdoor clothes, such as a long-sleeved shirt you always slip on. Anything you can do to make things regular and predictable will help you "fit in" with the creatures in your environment, so they will behave normally around you.

48 : WILDLIFE BLINDS

One spring, we purchased twelve sizable trees and planted them in the evening dim. Each tree was about four feet high. We called it the "instant forest." We looked on with pride. Oh, how the animals would love these trees!

A cardinal swooped downward. It pulled up sharply, almost smacked into one of the new trees, somersaulted in the air, and landed on the ground for a moment. A blue jay caught its wing tips on a branch and screeched. Squirrels circled, hawks swooped, and muskrats stared. Woodpeckers fluttered and floundered. Our instant forest had them, well, flustered. Wild animals have their daily routines, just as people do. If a huge tree sprang up in the road on your daily commute, I guess you'd be a bit startled, too!

Creating a Wildlife Blind

The fact that wild animals become accustomed to things—the placement of a tree, a chair, a table—can be used to a wildlife watcher's advantage. Scientists and wildlife photographers create blinds—structures that hide them from creatures' view. They construct small huts near nests and wildlife hotspots they want to observe. Soon, the animals don't notice the blind—or the human behind it. So the photographer or scientist can watch a wild animal without disturbing it. You can do the same.

A traditional wildlife blind is a small shack camouflaged with camouflage paint, brown cloth, or branches. A small wooden crate with slats does the job. So would a large cardboard box—but it won't last through many rains. The longer the blind is out in the habitat, the more the animals ignore it. So having an outdoor-proof blind helps.

The biggest issue for blinds is entering and leaving. Can entering and leaving be done from the back and done quietly? If you have to remove noisy branches or open a creaky door, you'll have to sit quietly longer until wildlife return. Sometimes, this is unavoidable. Enlist your children in coming up with creative designs to solve the entering and leaving problem.

The best wildlife blind is your house. A tree house, playhouse, porch, or gazebo can serve. Simply design lookouts, spots where you can peek through at animals. Avoiding noticeable motion is key. If peeking out of a curtain moves a whole large piece of cloth, then it's likely to disturb the creatures.

The Shape Blind

An official wildlife blind that fully blocks you from wildlife isn't necessary. Just making your shape part of another shape that animals are accustomed to seems to do the trick. When you sit in a chair, and your shape becomes part of the lawn set, you become less noticeable. Lawn chairs where you can stretch out are perfect for this. Benches with high backs are terrific. If you're part of a regular object, animals are likely to pass you by.

Even if there's a table that's always outside and part of the landscape, the birds get used to it. Just sitting at it, quietly, will help make you less disturbing. A chipmunk may dash past a table. What's a few more legs, in addition to chair legs, after all? It's when you stand out in the open that animals notice you.

In many national and state parks, cars act as blinds. Animals get used to cars passing by, or even stopping. But once the doors open and people step out of the car, the animals move away in concern. In our own driveway, I sometimes pull in and just watch the animals for a few moments. The woodpeckers stay on the suet, the goldfinches stay feeding on the cup plants until I emerge. What works as a blind in your neighborhood may be something entirely different. Like everything with wildlife watching, you just have to try and see what works.

49 : HANDS AND FEET AWARENESS

Young children—and distracted adults—can lose awareness of where their feet and hands are. That's a problem out in nature. Anywhere there's an on, under, in, or beside, there's a spot for scorpions, bees, and other biting and stinging creatures to hide. So it's best to look at where your feet are going and double-check before putting hands on logs or trees. This is especially true when stepping in rocky areas, on or over logs on trails, or settling in for a rest or picnic. Teaching children to have extra awareness of where their hands and feet are when they are in wild areas can help them enjoy nature without bumbling into problems.

With little ones, you can make a goofy outdoor game out of noticing where hands and feet are placed. Start with feet. Have all participants announce each foot, just before it touches the ground. Every step. If game players know left and right, they can specify that, as well. Prepare for a chorus of "Foot. Foot!" "Foot. Foot!"

Then add in hands. "Hand!" "Hand!"

Have participants walk, sit, or crawl while still announcing. It can be a silly game without a winner or loser. Or you can have whoever makes a mistake—placing a hand or foot without announcing—sit down, out of the game. Start a new game, then another, over and over again.

Of course, out in nature, you wouldn't want to scare off creatures by announcing every foot or hand. But looking to see, and noticing, where your limbs are is the key to moving through nature comfortably, and observing animals instead of accidentally squashing them or being stung by them.

If you have very young children, you may want a few special parts of your wildlife habitat to have signs or symbols to indicate the proper behavior in that area. Enlist the kids to help decide on the designated areas and signs or symbols. Maybe there's an area with spiny cactus where extra care with watching hands and feet is needed. Or an area with seedlings that need tending and not stepping on. Perhaps a bird is raising chicks, and that area needs a reminder to be extra quiet. Having designated quiet areas, fast-walking or slow-walking areas, or extra-care-with-hands-and-feet areas will give variety to the garden. Yet it will also allow kids freedom to be their rambunctious selves elsewhere.

If the kids take part in setting up the areas, they'll feel more ownership in adhering to the suggested behavior. Kindergartners take pride in having learned a rule and showing off that they know it. They may be eager to guide a neighbor, grandparent, aunt, or uncle on the path in order to tell them just how they should behave!

50 : WHAT ABOUT MOSQUITOES?

Not all wild creatures are fun to encounter. Mosquitoes can make spending time in one's garden unpleasant. There is no perfect solution for the mosquito issue, but here are some tips from our years of experience outdoors.

MAKE SURE THE WATER YOU HAVE IS FLOWING. If you have a water garden, and that water flows, or even ripples with a slow drip, it will discourage mosquitoes from laying eggs. That's why a bird bath with a dripper or a water garden with a recirculating pump works well. Our nearby natural stream flows, so that isn't a problem. If a still pond has fish, those should eat the mosquito larva. Check to see if you have standing water in tires, old buckets, or watering cans lying around a yard or shed. Pour these out.

PICK THE RIGHT TIMES TO BE ACTIVE IN THE GARDEN. In our area the most problematic mosquitoes (those that most often seem to carry disease) are those that are active in early evening. So we simply plan our gardening for earlier in the day. Yet there are many species of mosquitoes. Each has its own habits and habitat. Some weeks in summer, only the evening mosquitoes are active, or the mosquitoes only hang out in wet and shade. In our area, in early September, the midday, sunlight mosquitoes come out. They're almost impossible to escape.

WEAR LIGHT-COLORED LONG SLEEVES AND LONG SHIRTS DURING MOSQUITO-Y PARTS OF THE YEAR. Mosquitoes are attracted to dark clothes. Our car is the brown color of a herd animal, and mosquitoes and other biting insects noticeably swarm it, which makes getting out tricky. Note to self: buy different color car next time.

GO OUT AFTER RAIN. Mosquitoes are usually scarce after a rainstorm. (Again, it depends on the species.)

COVER YOUR NECK. Wear long hair down. It's natural mosquito protection. Teach your long-haired kids to unclip their hair and put it around their necks when they're in mosquito-y areas. Bandanas worn around the neck are handy for so many uses, and this is one. A bandana can be fluffed out a bit or flattened, to protect skin when entering a mosquito-rich area.

STAY IN THE SUN. Create wide trails or mowed areas adjacent to wildlife areas you like to observe. Most of the mosquito species in our region tend to hang out in shade, where shrubs and tall plants overhang a path. You and your kids can walk these wider trails and enjoy the insects, without being in the midst of them.

Waging War on Mosquitoes

Some people, annoyed by mosquitoes, wage war on them. The cost is high to wildlife, and the efforts are rarely fully successful. Purplish lights that attract insects and then zap them with electricity have, thankfully, gone out of fashion. The zapper contraptions indiscriminately kill all insects, including insects that prey on mosquitoes, so using them kills off the part of nature that is actually helping decrease mosquito populations! Along the way, an insect zapper will kill off dragonflies, luna moths, lightning bugs, and other incredible wild creatures, as well. We tried using a more recent mosquito control machine, the Mosquito Magnet, which is designed to attract and trap mosquitoes, but, despite the rave reviews and studies that proclaimed the product's usefulness, we didn't get any benefit from it; we found a lot of beneficial insects in the traps and very few mosquitoes.

Finally, it's helpful to remember that some people are far more attractive to mosquitoes than others. This is part of natural body chemistry and can vary from day to day, or year to year. Don't assume that just because you're not getting bitten, everyone else is fine. My husband, while he was taking a particular medicine one summer, was wildly attractive to mosquitoes, horseflies, and all manner of biting flies. I could walk the same trail and not get a bite because they flew behind him like a cloud. The point is, if one of your family is a magnet for mosquitoes, and says they are getting bitten, believe them.

51 : REACHING OUT TO THE COMMUNITY

Your patio, porch, schoolyard habitat, or yard needn't be the limit of your family's wildlife gardening efforts. Look beyond. Every neighborhood could use more plantings for wildlife—butterfly-attracting plants, berry bushes for birds, prairie grasses, prickly pear cacti, or trees. Even folks who aren't interested in wildlife might still appreciate some pretty flowers or a strong, shade-giving tree. Perhaps you have a neighbor who would love those things and has gardening space but doesn't have the time, money, know-how, or physical energy to invest in planting and watering. Check to see if your children's school has an outdoor science lab or a bit of gardening room that is in need. Share knowledge. Share plants and seeds. Your children can be diggers and helpers.

Perhaps your kids can form a green crew to find out neighbors' needs. Below are some ideas to incorporate wildlife gardening—you don't have to call it by that name—into the life of the greater community.

Celebrating and Commemorating with Plants

Many people hold the tradition of planting a tree to mark a special event, such as when a child is born or someone passes away. But imagine how many more events, such as community events, could be commemorated by tree planting—at schools, public buildings, and other spaces. You can help with what you've learned. Advocate for the planting of trees, and for the choice of trees that benefit local wildlife. Some state departments of environment and even city governments have free trees and grants to help fund public landscaping. A few have small "beautification grants" for planting flowers and trees in front yards. You and your kids, as a crew, can bring up this idea, get permission, and enact the plans.

If a tree isn't manageable, then a perennial butterfly-attracting plant or garden might suit for a birthday or anniversary or thank you. Or you could offer to plant a native cactus (or other thorny native plant) in honor of a friend experiencing a prickly event in their lives. (Break-ups? Chemotherapy? Midlife birthdays, anyone?) Like lemonade from lemons, the cactus flowers that bloom and the birds that visit them will transform the prickly event as time goes on. Just offer to be the one to plant the gift plant if your friend is not already a gardener, so the gift creates ease, not burden, and planting is done properly. Now that you've acquired knowledge, you can pass it on.

One note: plant several plants, whenever possible, especially in the case of trees. Sometimes trees die. Sometimes ice causes branches to break off. Sometimes a tree gets in the way of other plans. When my husband was fighting an illness, we planted three sycamore trees. We called them "sick-no-more" trees. He, and two of those trees, are thriving, but one sycamore was half-chewed by a deer and is looking, well, not so hot. We're glad that's not the only one we planted. If you're creating a symbol for a life, increase the odds for its success. Even better than planting a tree at birth would be to plant trees for every birthday and have an entire forest as we grow older in life. At least that would be my dream.

Building a Sensory Garden

About fifty years ago, my grandmother had a next-door neighbor who was losing her eyesight. Grandmother went over and planted a special sensory garden for her: fragrant roses, lavender, and mint, as well as lamb's ears and other fuzzy and smooth plants that are fun to caress. Perhaps you have someone in your life who would enjoy a garden built with wildlife in mind, but also with a thought for that person's special needs. Imagine the possibilities. A garden for plants that can be seen with fingers, that touch with fragrance, that make sounds in a

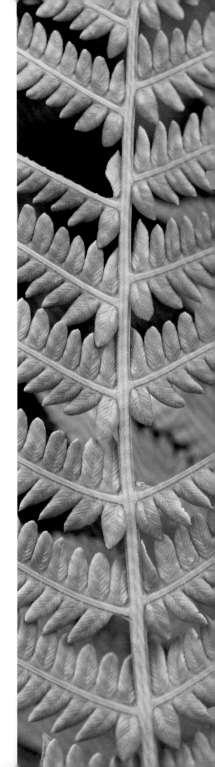

gentle breeze. A garden with sounds of splashes. How about a no-stoop garden, friendly to knees no longer so flexible? Or, a pathway that is wheelchair accessible?

To start your family's plan, research is in order. Thanks to the Internet, that can be quite easy. Search for the terms "sensory gardens" and "accessible garden." A sensory garden appeals to many senses, just as the name implies. Visit a local botanical garden and nature center for more ideas. The Chicago Botanic Garden and the Montréal Botanical Garden are among many sites that have beautiful sensory gardens. A botanical garden is likely to give you an idea of the shapes, colors, and types of plants that might be exciting for a garden. But botanical gardens feature a wide variety of plants from all over the world. Some are hard to care for and not appropriate for local yards, because they don't benefit local wildlife or they can escape from local gardens and damage wild areas. Your next step after researching plants for a sensory garden would be to search for native equivalents, appropriate to your area where possible.

Consult a knowledgeable local naturalist. Provide a photo of the plant, or even just the name, and ask for suggestions for good local, native equivalents that will benefit wildlife. You may find all sorts of options. Brainstorm your special garden with your family—the sky's the limit. A raised garden bed, commonly used in vegetable gardening, can be built for wildlife gardening, too. With raised beds, folks who cannot bend over easily can still reach the sensory plants or feel the breeze of butterfly wings and birds around them.

52 : GETTING YOUR WILDLIFE GARDEN CERTIFIED

As budding or ongoing wildlife gardeners, you and your family have considered the needs of wild animals and responded to them. You've begun to add wild habitat elements: food, water, shelter, and places for wildlife to raise young. You've invited wildlife to your yard, and, chances are, it's beginning to show up and fill your family's life with fluttering, flapping, scurrying fun. Seeing wildlife is already a reward for your efforts. But another satisfying way to honor what you've done is by getting your wildlife habitat certified.

The National Wildlife Federation and several other organizations provide certification for wildlife gardening. (See "Resources" for a list of organizations.) They have paper or online questionnaires that you fill out to tell about what you've provided for wildlife on your property. Wildlife gardening experts review what you've done, sometimes offer suggestions for next steps, and then give certification if you've put in good efforts. You don't need to wait until you've enacted all your plans or provided every habitat need to get your property certified. The organizations account for the fact that all wildlife gardeners are "in the process" of improving habitat.

Once your habitat is certified, you can obtain a certified wildlife habitat sign and display it proudly, to gently educate the neighbors walking by who may be wondering what you've been planting, all these years. By certifying your habitat, you've become part of a greater wild family—the thousands of people maintaining wildlife habitats in backyards, schoolyards, and business properties all over the United States, and elsewhere in the world.

Going Deeper: Your Family's Niche

One of the best things you can do for wildlife is to preserve really wild areas—vast tracts of undisturbed land for animals and plants to survive. Many creatures need these large patches of land, or they simply go extinct. But most of us don't have yards that big or yards on the edge of natural areas. So how can our yards help, other than providing a place for some "edgier" creatures to survive?

One way is by making our yards produce. Whatever food you can grow in your yard or neighborhood won't have to be trucked in from far away. Wild areas won't have to be made into farmland or set aside for chicken farming. I hadn't really thought about this directly until I read *Gaia's Garden: A Guide to Home-Scale Permaculture* by Toby Hemenway.

The practice of making your yard produce in this way is called "permaculture." It really looks at your yard as an entire system. It's a system that can provide shade, conserve water, produce food, and allow space for wildlife. We have already touched on some ways that vegetable gardens can be helpful for wildlife. But if you want to dig more deeply into sustaining your family and reducing your family's energy footprint on the Earth, I recommend you search out *Gaia's Garden* and other titles on permaculture. Perhaps some of the techniques can extend what your family is doing by integrating wildlife and the landscape into your lives.

Wild Families, Wild Gardens, Past and Future

Growing like weeds. Spreading like seeds. Branching like trees. Just a hundred years ago, most people on Earth would have had daily experiences with growing plants and would have understood these and hundreds of other metaphors. Yet today, children who have no experience with gardening miss out on connections not just to nature but also to culture—art, philosophy, even math—written with metaphors of nature in mind.

By getting your children out into nature, you're building those bridges between them and all the people on Earth who have ever experienced nature. Sun, wind, rain, seeds—an understanding of nature acts as a common language between people of different cultures and times. As you reach out to your community with your plants, seeds, and newfound gardening skills, you're helping others to connect as well. Hopefully, your work has also deepened your personal connection to nature and provided some laughter, learning, and memories for you and your kids. At the same time you have the satisfaction of knowing you're helping raise new birds, butterflies, frogs, and toads for the world.

Someday, you may have to give up a garden. Hurricanes, tornadoes, health and economic changes—they all shift us. Gardeners feel these moves root-tug-awful fierce. Some of the experiences I've written about in this book come from such a garden. Remembering it is both painful and sweet.

So what do we do? About losing wildlife gardens, about having to walk away? One way to make the loss less painful is to give away divisions and seeds from your land to neighbors and friends before you leave the property. Take some of the plants' offspring with you if you're moving to a similar habitat.

Mourn a bit. But know that a wildlife garden is never a waste. For a time, your garden was a refuge. You created a preserve for biodiversity. Many of the seeds, the animals you supported, will move on, perhaps find another haven with someone else. Yes, permanently preserved areas are best. But a network of shifting, changing patches of wildlife gardens can also be valuable. They help wildlife build up numbers and spread to new areas. This is a service, too.

This all sounds so serious. Okay, it is. But at the same time, it's simple, muddy, messy. Wildlife gardening is the good stuff. In a world where people who love nature can get tired out with news and statistics, the wildlife garden is a place where we restore ourselves and nature. It provides spontaneous moments where you and your kids focus in, breath held, to watch a squirrel carefully fluffing and grooming its tail or a mother bird feeding a caterpillar to her nestling. It's a place for joy and growth. On behalf of plants and seeds and wild creatures that can't send thank you notes, Jeff and I thank you for all you're doing, for all you're sharing, for all you're growing on your particular patch of earth.

Acknowledgments

Thank you, Jeff, for reviewing the manuscript and contributing important changes. Thank you to the Hive writers and to Donnie, Andrea, Candace, Barb, George, dear friends who assisted during many of our gardening adventures. Thanks to Sara St. Antoine of the Children & Nature Network for reading and giving me early feedback. A special hug for Liz Cunningham, for keeping my spirits up during this project. Thank you, Dr. Philip C. Rosen of the University of Arizona, for the desert toad advice. Thanks and a hello wave to the former NatureScope crew (Judy, Luise, Ellen, Sara, Jodi, Cindy, Debby, Kim) and all the Ranger Rick and National Wildlife Federation folks (Craig Tufts!) who nurtured my writing and wildlife knowledge at the beginning of my career and who have contributed so much to nature education in their separate travels and work since those early days.

Resources

Books about Gardening

Hemenway, Toby. *Gaia's Garden: A Guide to Home-Scale Permaculture.* White River Junction, Vt.: Chelsea Green, 2009.

Miller, George Oxford. *Landscaping with Native Plants of the Southwest.* St. Paul, Minn.: Voyageur, 2007.

Roth, Sally. *Attracting Butterflies and Hummingbirds to Your Backyard: Watch Your Garden Come Alive with Beauty on the Wing.* Emmaus, Pa.: Rodale, 2001.

Seidenberg, Charlotte. *The Wildlife Garden: Planning Backyard Habitats.* Jackson: University of Mississippi, 1995.

Tallamy, Douglas W. *Bringing Nature Home: How Native Plants Sustain Wildlife in Our Gardens.* Portland, Ore.: Timber, 2007.

Xerces Society. *Xerxes Society Guide to Attracting Native Pollinators: Protecting North America's Bees and Butterflies,* ed. Deborah Burns. North Adams, Mass.: Storey Publishing, 2011.

Books about Nature Play and Education

Christopher, Todd. *The Green Hour: A Daily Dose of Nature for Happier, Healthier, Smarter Kids.* Boston: Roost Books, 2010.

Keeler, Rusty. *Natural Playscapes: Creating Outdoor Play Environments for the Soul.* Redmond, Wash.: Exchange, 2008.

Louv, Richard. *Last Child in the Woods: Why Children Need Nature, How It Was Taken from Them, and How to Get It Back.* Chapel Hill, N.C.: Algonquin of Chapel Hill, 2005.

———. *The Nature Principle: Human Restoration and the End of Nature-Deficit Disorder.* Chapel Hill, N.C.: Algonquin of Chapel Hill, 2011.

Sobel, David. *Wild Play: Parenting Adventures in the Great Outdoors.* San Francisco: Sierra Club, 2011.

Stone, Michæl K., and Zenobia Barlow. *Ecological Literacy: Educating Our Children for a Sustainable World.* San Francisco: Sierra Club, 2005.

Ward, Jennifer. *I Love Dirt! 52 Activities to Help You and Your Kids Discover the Wonders of Nature.* Boston: Roost Books, 2008.

Field Guides for Wildlife Watching and Wildflowers

Beadle, David, and Leckie Seabrook. *Peterson Field Guide to Moths of Northeastern North America*. New York: Houghton Mifflin, 2012.

Behrstock, Robert A. *Dragonflies and Damselflies of the Southwest*. Tucson, Ariz.: Rio Nuevo, 2008.

Benyus, Janine M. *The Field Guide to Wildlife Habitats of the Eastern United States*. New York: Simon & Schuster, 1989.

———. *The Field Guide to Wildlife Habitats of the Western United States*. New York: Simon & Schuster, 1989.

———. *Northwoods Wildlife: A Watcher's Guide to Habitats*. Minocqua, Wis.: NorthWord, 1989.

Bowers, Nora, Rick Bowers, and Kenn Kaufman. *Kaufman Field Guide to Mammals of North America*. New York: Houghton Mifflin, 2007.

Conant, Roger, and Joseph T. Collins. *A Field Guide to Reptiles and Amphibians: Eastern and Central North America*. Boston: Houghton Mifflin, 1998.

Dunkle, Sidney W. *Dragonflies through Binoculars: A Field Guide to Dragonflies of North America*. New York: Oxford University, 2000.

Eaton, Eric R., and Kenn Kaufman. *Kaufman Field Guide to Insects of North America*. New York: Houghton Mifflin, 2007.

Eiseman, Charley, Noah Charney, and John Carlson. *Tracks and Signs of Insects and Other Invertebrates: A Guide to North American Species*. Mechanicsburg, Pa.: Stackpole, 2010.

Glassberg, Jeffrey. *Butterflies through Binoculars: The East*. New York: Oxford University Press, 1999.

———. *Butterflies through Binoculars: The West: A Field Guide to the Butterflies of Western North America*. Oxford: Oxford University Press, 2001.

Kaufman, Kenn. *Guía de campo a las aves de norteamérica*. Boston: Houghton Mifflin, 2005.

———. *Lives of North American Birds*. Boston: Houghton Mifflin, 1996.

Kaufman, Kenn, Rick Bowers, Nora Bowers, and Lynn Hassler. *Kaufman Field Guide to Birds of North America*. New York: Houghton Mifflin, 2005.

Kenney, Leo P., and Matthew R. Burne. *A Field Guide to the Animals of Vernal Pools*. Westborough, Mass.: Massachusetts Division of Fisheries & Wildlife, Natural Heritage & Endangered Species Program, 2000.

Newcomb, Lawrence. *Newcomb's Wildflower Guide*. Boston: Little, Brown, 1977.

Niering, William A., and Nancy C. Olmstead. *National Audubon Society Field Guide to North American Wildflowers: Eastern Region*. New York: Alfred A. Knopf, 2000.

Paulson, Dennis R. *Dragonflies and Damselflies of the East*. Princeton, N.J.: Princeton University Press, 2011.

Peterson, Roger Tory. *Peterson Field Guide to Birds of North America*. Boston: Houghton Mifflin, 2008.

Sibley, David, Chris Elphick, and John B. Dunning. *The Sibley Guide to Bird Life and Behavior*. New York: Alfred A. Knopf, 2009.

Wagner, David L. *Caterpillars of Eastern North America: A Guide to Identification and Natural History.* Princeton, N.J.: Princeton University Press, 2005.

Wright, Amy. *Peterson First Guides Caterpillars: The Concise Field Guide to 120 Common Caterpillars of North America.* New York: Houghton Mifflin, 1993.

Children's Books

Collard, Sneed B. *The Prairie Builders: Reconstructing America's Lost Grasslands.* Boston: Houghton Mifflin, 2005.

Macken, JoAnn Early, and Pamela Paparone. *Flip, Float, Fly: Seeds on the Move.* New York: Holiday House, 2008.

Mikula, Rick. *The Family Butterfly Book.* North Adams, Mass.: Storey, 2000.

Sayre, April Pulley, and Barbara Bash. *Dig, Wait, Listen: A Desert Toad's Tale.* New York: Greenwillow, 2001.

Sayre, April Pulley, and Kate Endle. *Trout Are Made of Trees.* Watertown, Mass.: Charlesbridge, 2008.

Sayre, April Pulley, and Patricia Wynne. *The Bumblebee Queen.* Watertown, Mass.: Charlesbridge, 2005.

Sayre, April Pulley, and Trip Park. *Ant, Ant, Ant!: An Insect Chant.* Minnetonka, Minn.: NorthWord for Young Readers, 2005.

Schæfer, Lola M., and Donald Crews. *This Is the Sunflower.* New York: Greenwillow, 2000.

Schæfer, Lola M., and Gabi Swiatkowska. *Arrowhawk.* New York: Henry Holt, 2004.

St. Antoine, Sara. *Stories from Where We Live* series. Minneapolis, Minn.: Milkweed Editions, 2000—2006.

Stewart, Melissa, and Higgins Bond. *A Place for Butterflies.* Atlanta: Peachtree, 2006.

Websites for Wildlife Gardening, Wildlife Watching, and Nature Education

www.nwf.org
The National Wildlife Federation Certified Wildlife Habitat Program is the oldest, most comprehensive program of its kind available. The website is full of helpful wildlife gardening information.

www.childrenandnature.org
The Children & Nature Network is the best web resource for books, videos, activities, and links related to children and nature. It has information on forming a nature club for kids, community forums for connecting to others interested in nature, scholarly information related to the importance of children having time outdoors, and resources such as a free downloadable information kit, "Together in Nature: Pathways to a Stronger, Closer Family."

http://getoutside.audubon.org
The National Audubon Society's "Get Outside" program offers website information on wildlife garden-ing and a directory of the Audubon centers where you can take classes, experience the outdoors, and get information on wildlife gardening.

www.ahs.org
The American Horticultural Society has a conference on youth gardening and materials regarding build-ing children's gardens.

www.arborday.org
The Arbor Day Foundation and the Dimensions Educational Research Foundation have a "Nature Ex-plore" program that has plans for outdoor spaces, consultants to help design schoolyard habitats, certifica-tion for Nature Explore classrooms, and many other outdoor environmental education resources.

www.azgfd.gov
The Arizona Fish and Game Department provides publications about wildlife gardening in desert envi-ronments.

www.batcon.org
Bat Conservation International provides bat information and links to sites that sell bat houses.

http://captainplanetfoundation.org
Captain Planet gives grants for environmental programs such as schoolyard and community wildlife gardens.

www.dbg.org
The Phoenix Desert Botanical Garden has a huge wildlife gardening display and native plant sales. Their website hosts information about southwestern native plants and wildlife gardening.

www.desertmuseum.org
The Arizona—Sonora Desert Museum displays native plants and animals and provides wildlife informa-tion for the Tucson area. Their Center for Sonoran Studies has classes for kids and adults.

www.desertusa.com/wildflo/wildupdates.html
Desert USA is a commercial travel site with information about the Southwest. It hosts yearly updates on when wildflowers bloom in Arizona, California, New Mexico, Utah, Texas, and Oregon.

www.wildones.org/seedmony.htm
The Lorrie Otto Seeds for Education Grant Program is managed by the Wild Ones organization and gives small cash grants to schools and nature centers to build wildlife gardens.

www.greeneducationfoundation.org
The Green Education Foundation runs a program called "Green Thumb Challenge" with information and funds for schoolyard gardens.

www.iwla.org
The Izaak Walton League teaches stream monitoring through its Save Our Streams program.

www.jmgkids.us
Through this site, the National Wildlife Federation and the Junior Master Gardener Program together offer certification for young gardeners as an offshoot of master gardener certification. Also on the site, the American Horticultural Society has a list of "classic" children's books related to gardening and awards a yearly Growing Good Kids Excellence in Children's Literature award.

www.kellogghubbard.org/storywalk.html
This site contains information on the StoryWalk™ program for using books as signs for nature trails and community walk events.

www.learner.org/jnorth
Journey North is a website for classrooms to follow the migration of creatures and blooming of plants.

www.naturerocks.org
At the Nature Rocks website, you can enter your city, state, and zip code to find out about nature activities in your area.

www.macaulaylibrary.org
The Macaulay Library of Sounds at the Cornell Lab of Ornithology is a source for downloads and CDs of animal calls.

www.monarchwatch.org
Monarch Waystation Program is an educational outreach program based at the University of Kansas and focuses on plantings for monarchs, to support monarch migration. The website offers detailed information on monarch life cycles and milkweed species.

www.nabluebirdsociety.org
The North American Bluebird Society provides information on bluebird houses and how to maintain them.

www.plantnative.com
The PlantNative website has information and links to native plant nurseries throughout the United States.

www.pollinator.org
The Pollinator Partnership provides great educational materials including planting guides with specific plant recommendations for each region of the U.S.

www.projectnoah.org
Project Noah is an Internet resource that enables sharing nature sightings with people worldwide

www.projectwild.org
Project Wild and Project Wild Aquatic, programs of the Council of Environmental Education, provide curriculum resources and workshops to teachers working with students on nature study. This is one of the longest running, most widely used environmental study programs.

http://purplemartin.org
The Purple Martin Conservation Association provides information on attracting and maintaining purple martin colonies.

http://research.amnh.org/burroughs/young_readers_list.html
The John Burroughs Association of the American Natural History Museum gives a yearly award to outstanding natural history books for children. Their book list is on this site.

www.wildflower.org
The Lady Bird Johnson Wildflower Center in Austin, Texas, is a prime source for wildflower information. It offers exhibits, classes, seed grants, and all kinds of resources for native plant gardeners. The organization's website has links to native plant lists and native plant suppliers nationwide.

www.wildsanctuary.com
A source for downloads and CDs of animal calls from Bernie Krause, a world-renowned sound expert and recordist.

State and Regional Wildlife Gardening Organizations

Some states and state or regional organizations also offer certifications in landscaping for wildlife. For instance, the University of Florida Wildlife Extension service certifies backyard habitats (www.wec.ufl .edu/extension/landscaping/fblw/). Search online for your own state's name together with the search term "wildlife gardening" to see if any programs are available for your area. Southeastern gardeners should definitely check out the site maintained by the Environmental Education Alliance of Georgia (www .eealliance.org); they offer a certification tailored for native pollinator gardens.

Credits

Perhaps it takes a village not only to raise a child but sometimes, also, to complete a book. To create this book, Jeff and I offered up our decades of wildlife gardening and nature photos. But this project did not become real until family, friends, educators, and school communities I had visited stepped forward to contribute photos of their children experiencing nature and wildlife gardening. It still moves me when I remember the hundreds of family joy/classroom discovery moments that showed up in my inbox. Heartfelt thanks to all.

Many photos came courtesy of the Gordon School, a racially diverse nursery through eighth grade school in East Providence, Rhode Island. The Phoenix Desert Botanical Garden allowed me to photograph on their grounds. Thank you to Michelle Cusolito of the Polliwog on Safari blog (http://michellecusolito.blogspot.com) for use of photos. Thank you to Jane Naliboff (www.jane naliboff.com) for the blue eggs photo and robin nestlings photo. Here are the other folks who generously contributed photos, whether the images were used or not (we only wish more images had fit into the book): Geoff Griffin, the Edible Schoolyard Project, children's book author JoAnn Early Macken (www. joannmacken.com), the Egan family, the Griffith family, the Noyce family, the Musgrave family, the Walatka family, the McAdam family, the Willett family, the Rogers family, the Acerro family, the Crighton family, the Donahue family, the Ballard family, the Partlow family, the Fox family, the Kaufhold family, the Ottewell family, the Long family, children's book author Lyn Sirota (www.lynsirota .com), children's book author Faythe Thureen, educator Lyn Hartman, and teachers Jacqui Ketner, Neville Motta, Shai Pina, and Kate Mercurio.

Index

fences, 102—103, 105
fertilizers, 126
field guides, 44—45
firewood, 27
fish, for water gardens, 97—98
flowers, 105—106, 111, 116, 128, 160—161. *See also* wildflowers
food sources, for wildlife, 28—30
forests, as layered habitats, 15—16. *See also* tree(s)
frogs, 31, 93, 96, 97
Frost, Helen, 154
fruit, 117—118, 141—143, 148—149. *See also* berries

Glassberg, Jeffrey, 109
Google Maps, 51, 55
Graber, Jean, 157
Graber, Richard, 157
grasses, native, 40, 100—101. *See also* native plants

hawks, 21—23, 24, 34, 55—56, 176
hearing-impaired individuals. *See* disabled individuals
hedgerows, 40—41
Hemenway, Toby, 190
hide-and-seek, 24
hideouts, 22—23
homeschoolers, 57
hummingbirds, 8, 15, 30, 37, 43, 80, 153, 158—162

interplanting, 69
invasive plants, 75—76

jewelweed, 153
journals. *See* notebooks, nature

Kaufman, Kenn, 45
Krause, Bernie, 8

lawns, mowing, 99—101
layered habitats, 23—24
lichen, 167
lint. *See* dryer lint
listening, 7—8
log piles, 26—27
lookout spots, 24, 92, 122. *See also* perches
lupine, 154

Macken, JoAnn Early, 154
mapping, 43—44, 51—57
mealworms, 157
migration, 55—57, 103, 112, 116
Mikula, Rick, 109
milkweed, 154, 155
Miller, George Oxford, 82
mites, 19
mosquitoes, 130, 182—184
moths, 39, 130
mud rooms, 11—12

native plants, 40, 74—78, 81, 97, 100—101, 125, 142—143
nests, 42—45, 163—170
notebooks, nature, 5—6, 29, 31, 48, 51, 62, 111
nut trees, 148—149

oak trees, 84, 86, 157

parasites, 17, 75

pathways, animal, 55—57. *See also* migration
pears, 148. *See also* fruit
perches, 38, 125. *See also* lookout spots
percolation test, 62
permaculture, 190
pesticides, 32, 99
photographs. *See* digital cameras
pile shelters, 25—27
plant(s)
    for butterfly gardens, 115—118
    celebrating/commemorating with, 186—187
    grouping, 81
    invasive, 75—76
    native, 40, 74—78, 81, 97, 100—101, 125, 142—143
    pioneering, 75—76
    planting/transplanting, 69, 71—73, 81—82
    preparing the ground for, 68—70
    for water gardens, 97
pollen, 115—116
pollination, 27, 160
pollutants, 32, 126
puddles, 134—135

railroad lines, 56—57
rain, 9—12, 15, 183
raised beds, 188
raspberries, 146. *See also* berries
recording sounds, 8. *See also* sound
Ryder, Joanne, 134

About the Author

APRIL PULLEY SAYRE is an award-winning author of sixty children's books including *Trout Are Made of Trees*, *The Bumblebee Queen*, and *Rah, Rah, Radishes: A Vegetable Chant*. Her book *Vulture View* received ALA's Theodor "Seuss" Geisel Honor Award. *Stars beneath Your Bed: The Surprising Story of Dust* won the AAAS/Subaru SB&F Prize for Excellence. Sayre is a three-time winner of the John Burroughs Award for nature writing for young people. She and her husband, Jeff, coauthored a natural history of hummingbirds called *Hummingbirds: The Sun Catchers*. Jeff Sayre is the coauthor of *The Kaufman Field Guide to Nature of the Midwest*.

April Pulley Sayre began her career working at the National Wildlife Federation and the National Geographic Society. Now, as a full-time author and speaker, she shares her rain-forest adventures, wildlife gardening knowledge, and the nonfiction writing process with twenty thousand children and educators each year during school visits and workshops nationwide. April and Jeff, who for five years was director of a native-plant nursery, live and garden in the Midwest. More information on their work and additional wildlife gardening links can be found at www.aprilsayre.com.